The

# BOSTON
# FISH
# PIER

## Seafood Recipe
## Cook Book

$\mathcal{D}$

**Doyle Studio Press • Watertown, Massachusetts**

First Doyle Studio Press Edition 1996

Published in the United States by Doyle Studio Press,
Watertown, Massachusetts

10 9 8 7 6 5 4 3 2 1

Printed in the United States of America

The

# BOSTON
# FISH
# PIER

Seafood Recipe
Cook Book

# INTRODUCTION

In a city full of wonderful contrasts, the Boston Fish Pier remains one of the special places that defines Boston. Not yet ready to become a remnant of a once great fishing industry, the pier is a place that is still full of life, even well before sunrise. The cold, salty breeze from the harbor, the cucumber smell of fresh fish, the weatherworn faces, the buzz of yelling, laughter, profanity, and friendly conversation—the place in rich in aroma, sound, color, language, humanity—it is quintessential Boston.

Lots of wheeling and dealing.

Activities each morning build to a crescendo as the buyers and fishing boat captains gather in the auction room. A large chalkboard lists the boats and their catch—in thousand pound increments—by species. The auction begins and within the hour all the fish will be sold, then loaded onto empty trucks and rushed to be processed and shipped to restaurants and markets throughout New England—and nearly every corner of the world.

When the New England Fish Exchange was formed in 1908 "to maintain a room for the purchase and sale of fish," the annual catch from the New England states was more than 500,000,000 pounds! The fishing industry, which created the wealth that New England's economy was founded upon, had already been eclipsed by textiles and other new industries, but was still a major employer and economic force. At its inception, the Boston Fish Pier was the "best appointed" facility of its type in the world. Built of cement, brick, and glazed tile, it was designed to be "thoroughly hygienic" and "fireproof." It was 537,100 square feet—second only to Grimsby, England in size, and was able to unload eighty fishing vessels at one time. (Today there are less than forty boats in the entire fleet.) The new pier had its own power plant, cold storage facility, administration building, and two large buildings housing forty-four fish stores. The New England fishing industry was vibrant and it was basking in the glory of its new world-class fish pier.

One very successful company, Freeman & Cobb Co., Inc., famous for its Wachusett brand of "haddies" (Finnan Haddie), commissioned Mary J. Lincoln, the very well-known author, cooking teacher, and principal of the Boston Cooking-School (prior to Fannie Merritt Farmer), to create recipes for Wachusett Haddies. The recipes were probably published in 1908 as a booklet. Later, in 1913, Freeman & Cobb presented *Recipes for Sea Food* by J. H. Griffin, with Mary J. Lincoln's haddie recipes at the back of the book. Other large seafood companies, such as Gorton's, followed suit by printing recipe booklets for the purpose of promoting and educating the public about seafood. But this rare volume—reproduced here in its original form—remains the most comprehensive seafood cookbook of its era.

The book begins with "an expert treatise on fish as food." I thoroughly enjoyed this section, delighting in the wide assortment of factual information, as well as the timely comments on almost every facet of seafood, from fishing techniques to mentions of under appreciated species, such as hake and sea robins. I'm not qualified to comment on the accuracy of the nutritional information, but I am duly impressed with the extent and seriousness with which it tackles this subject. When *Recipes for Sea Food* was first published, seafood was considered by many to be inferior to meat as a source of protein. Fish was brain food—fine for college professors, white-collar workers, women, and children. For many, it was mandatory on Friday and acceptable on occasion, but on a daily basis, meat was still considered the necessary fuel for a man engaged in manual labor. This book defies the conventional wisdom of its time and makes a case for fish as an excellent source of protein, carbohydrates, fat, and calories. It also analyzes the low price of this nutritious food when compared to meat. (And it supplies very official looking charts to back up its message.) In short, it is a wonderfully presented sales pitch for the fishing industry. Additionally, the opening section is peppered with all kinds of useful information on yields, storage, sanitation, cooking techniques, and equipment. It even has a small glossary of cooking terminology and extracts from *The Fish and Game Laws of Massachusetts*, 1912.

Because little is known of the author of record, J. H. Griffin, I can only speculate about the origins of these recipes. It is entirely possible that J. H. Griffin did create and write this original manuscript, but I have doubts. She (American men did not write recipes in this era) most certainly compiled the information and recipes, but the repertoire and recipes themselves have a very distinct resemblance to the teachings of the Boston Cooking-School. Give the fact that the "presenter"—Freeman & Cobb Co.—already had a business relationship with Mary J. Lincoln and included her recipes in the back of this book, it seems a bit unlikely that they would seek another source for recipes. After all, Mary J. Lincoln was quite well known at this time — equally as famous as Fannie Merritt Farmer. She preceded Fannie Farmer as principal of the Boston Cooking-School, and her book, *Mrs. Lincoln's Boston Cook Book*, was said to have been freely borrowed from by Fannie Farmer whose book, *The Boston Cooking-School Cook Book*, became a timeless classic. In *Recipes for Sea Food*, the lingo, style and even the typeface greatly resembles that of Mary J. Lincoln and Fannie M. Farmer, divas of the "home economist" movement at the turn of the century. The recipes are simple, straightforward, and precise. However, they assume a fairly high level of knowledge from the cook. Maybe J. H. Griffin was a disciple of the Boston Cooking-School. Or maybe Mary Lincoln sold rights to these recipes to Freeman & Cobb and simply wasn't acknowledged. It remains a bit of a mystery.

The cooking of New England in 1913 was still based on English cooking, with a sprinkling of French cuisine. The repertoire was fairly standard; recipes might have varied slightly from author to author, but the dishes were mostly the same. And the writing was not descriptive at all. It was common for cookbooks from this era to list several recipes for the same dish, without any indication of preference or even a suggestion about the uses for the different variations. This book lists six different recipes for cod balls, five for fish chowder, and three for baked mackerel, four for broiled halibut, six for broiled oysters, five for creamed oysters, five for fried oysters, five for scalloped oysters, three for clam chowder, six for lobster newburg, four for lobster stew, and dozens of other recipes have two versions (usually called No. 1 and No. 2). This kind of detached, scientific presentation, makes it difficult to detect a personal style that would set one author's recipes apart from another's. For all these reasons I am also certain that—whether J. H. Griffin was the author, compiler, editor, creator or borrower—in one form or another, the wonderful recipes in this book have roots at the Boston Cooking-School.

For the most part, the instructions given in *Recipes for Sea Food* are still accurate and valid today. And the collection, with recipes for almost forty species of fish and shellfish, reflects the sophistication that seafood cookery had reached in Boston at the turn of the 19th century.

There are more than ninety recipes for oysters alone! Recipes range from the very basic—baked, broiled, fried, poached, roasted, and steamed seafood with little fuss—to complex classic dishes like Palmettes of Striped Bass, Chartreuse of Sole, and Lobster á la Bonnefoy from the Waldorf-Astoria Hotel in New York City.

The book contains many regional American preparations such as Cape Ann Chowder, Tongues and Sounds (cod tongues and cheeks), Crab Gumbo, Planked Shad, and Fried Catfish, but also includes a number of exotic dishes that sound as if they were taken off recent menus from Boston's hot new restaurants —Bluefish with Sweet Pepper Butter, Lobster with Hominy Croustade, or Griddled Oysters on Rye Shortcake. Several recipes use curry powder, which had been popular in Boston since the days of the clipper ships. And on the esoteric side, there are recipes for frog's legs, terrapin, smelts, sardines, eels, and other oddities like Veal Forcemeat (for stuffing fish) and a Norwegian Fish Pudding.

As a professional chef, I find this book full of good ideas and great flavor combinations, but as I mentioned earlier, the recipes speak to a more advanced audience than most modern cookbooks. The amounts given seem fairly accurate but the directions are very brief. Recipes that take five lines here would probably take a full page in a modern cookbook. If you are a good home cook, you will be able to make fabulous dishes from this book. Spend a little extra time to think through the recipe and then makes changes as you see fit. Recipes based on cream sauces, egg liaisons, and salt pork will need adjusting or they will be too rich for modern palates. Remember, when this book was written, these rich additions were thought to improve the nutritional value of the "lean" seafood. Similarly, the Chinese sometimes use rich, often meat based sauces, to fortify seafood dishes.

If you are just beginning to cook, skip over the more complex dishes. You will still find a wealth of information in this book. Start with salads, sandwiches, canapés or maybe even a soup. Or just kick back and read it for fun. Anyone who likes food will enjoy this vintage cookbook. It is humorous the way it wanders at times, throwing in comments about mutton or turkey or cooking times for vegetables.

I first heard of *Recipes for Sea Food* from Kevin Doyle, the publisher of this facsimile edition and owner of the only original copy (that we know of) of this book. I have been fascinated with it every since, picking it up dozens of times and always finding something new, clever, odd, or exciting. It is a welcome addition to my library—a book I intend to revisit and cook from often. I hope you will enjoy this book as much as I have and as you read it, as you cook from it, that you will experience, first hand, a sense of connection to our culinary past.

Jasper White
*Boston*
*September 1996*

# RECIPES
# FOR SEA FOOD

HOW TO PREPARE AND SERVE

## FISH, OYSTERS, CLAMS, SCALLOPS, LOBSTERS, CRABS, AND SHRIMP

*Containing in Addition*

AN EXPERT TREATISE ON FISH AS A FOOD — ADVICE TO
THE COOK—TIME TABLES FOR COOKING—TABLES OF
MEASURES AND PROPORTIONS—RULES FOR THE
KITCHEN—TERMS USED IN COOKING—PRAC-
TICAL POINTS — HOUSEHOLD HINTS—
EXTRACTS FROM THE GAME
LAWS OF MASSACHUSETTS

———

*PRESENTED BY*

## FREEMAN & COBB CO.

### BOSTON, MASS.

# BOSTON FISH MARKET CORPORATION

LESSEES of New Commonwealth Wharf in South Boston, a cut of which will be found on cover, built especially and to be used exclusively for the fresh fish business. Made entirely of cement, brick and glazed tile, thoroughly hygienic, in keeping with requirements of Board of Health, and fireproof.

Provides dock berths for forty vessels and can unload from eighty Vessels at same time. Contains an Administration Building and Cold Storage and Power Plant, and two long buildings containing forty-four fish stores. The entire property comprises 537,100 square feet.

Spur tracks on our property will make railroad facilities ample to all parts of the country.

Governor Draper, realizing the value of the industry to his State, was principal factor in getting the lease.

The property is the best appointed, and second in size only to Grimsby, England, of any fish market in the world.

# NEW ENGLAND FISH EXCHANGE

FORMED September, 1908, to maintain a room for the purchase and sale of fish, guaranteeing the consummation of all sales and purchases registered with it, serving both dealers and captains of vessels. Through its various channels it aims to better all conditions of the industry. Acts as clearing agency for all dealers and matters in general pertaining to the business.

We will be glad to co-operate with the Health Board of any section to prevent the sale of bad fish.

W. K. BEARDSLEY, *Manager.*

# WHOLESALE FISH DEALERS' CREDIT ASSOCIATION

OWING to the magnitude of the business as represented from a financial standpoint, the large and varied territory over which it expands, it became imperative to safeguard as far as possible the individual and collective interests of all the dealers and to that end the "Wholesale Fish Dealers' Credit Association" (two departments, Credit and Collection) was formed.

Its additional purpose also is to protect the honest retailer, so far as lies in its power, against the competition of the unscrupulous and designing who do not pay their honest obligations.

It is advisable, when seeking credit, to file with the association a statement on blanks provided for this purpose. These statements are affirmed or denied by our Correspondents who represent the association in all parts of this country and Canada. Such references qualify or deny the seeker to an open account.

Delinquents or "slow pay" are put on a cash basis.

Unscrupulous retailers or those who by design or sharp practice do not meet their honest obligations, arrangements are perfected for their prosecution. The compiled records, both credit and undesirables, are open to the inspection of all the dealers, hence it behooves any and all retailers to observe the one golden maxim, *i.e.*, "Honesty is the Best Policy."

While yet in its infancy, the association has demonstrated its worth, proven a valuable adjunct to our line, and has received many flattering testimonials from different business sections of the country.

B. A. DOHERTY, *Manager.*

# CONTENTS

# INDEX OF RECIPES

## FISH

# INDEX OF RECIPES

## FISH AND MEAT SAUCES

## OYSTERS

# CLAMS

# SCALLOPS

# LOBSTERS

# CRABS

# SHRIMPS

THE OLD TYPE OF FISHING SCHOONER

THE NEW TYPE OF FISHING SCHOONER

# FISH AS FOOD.

## INTRODUCTION.

### VALUE AND USE OF FISH.

As ordinarily used, the term fish includes, besides the fish proper, many other water animals, as oysters, clams, and other mollusks; lobsters, crawfish, crabs, and shrimps, and turtle and terrapin. The term "sea food" is often used to cover the whole group, or, more particularly, salt-water food products as distinguished from those of fresh water.

Fish in one form or another is almost universally recognized as an important food material, and enters to some extent into the diet of very many if not the majority of American families. Few, however, have any adequate conception of the great importance of the fisheries of the United States and of the immense amount of nutritive material which is every year taken from the salt and fresh waters of this country.

From recent data collected by the United States Fish Commission it appears that more than 528,000,000 pounds of fish, crustaceans, etc., are annually taken from the waters of the New England States; over 819,000,000 pounds from the Middle Atlantic States; over 106,000,000 from the South Atlantic States; 113,000,000 from the Gulf States; 217,000,000 from the Pacific coast; 96,000,000 from the Mississippi River and its tributaries, and 166,000,000 pounds from Alaska. The products of the fisheries of the Great Lakes exceed 113,000,000 pounds annually, and of the minor interior waters 5,000,000 pounds. In addition, thousands of pounds of fish are annually caught by sportsmen, but statistics of the amount are not available. In the case of the coast sections the statistics given above include only the coast fisheries. The interior fisheries of Vermont are included with those of New England, the fisheries of New York and Pennsylvania on the Great Lakes with those of the Middle Atlantic States, and the fish-

eries of the east coast of Florida with those of the Gulf States.
The data for the Great Lakes embrace only those States not
having coast fisheries, but include the fisheries of the Ohio
River for Ohio, Indiana, and Illinois. The figures for the
interior States are confined to States not having coast or Great
Lake fisheries. In all sections the data represent the products
as they leave the hands of the fishermen, except that in the
case of Alaska the figures include salmon after being canned
or otherwise prepared for the market. In considering such
products as clams, scallops, and oysters the weight of the
edible portion only has been taken into account.

The total weight of the fish products of the United States
as they leave the hands of the fishermen is about 2,169,000,000
pounds, representing in round numbers as the value of the
catch $58,000,000. By the processes of canning, salting,
smoking, and otherwise preserving, the value of the fish is
very much increased.

Of the very large quantity of fish annually placed on the
American market, the greater part is consumed at home,
although a portion is prepared in various ways for export.

The preference for fresh-water or salt-water fish is a matter
of individual taste. Both are, so far as known, equally wholesome. Indeed, it may be said that in general the preference
for one kind of sea food or another is quite largely a matter of
circumstances. It is noticeable that many kinds of fish which
are known to be good for food are seldom eaten. Among
others may be mentioned the whiting, or silver hake, and the
sea robin. The latter are taken in enormous quantities in
certain regions. This prejudice against certain fish is largely
local; for instance, skates are eaten on the western coast of
the United States, but until recently they were regarded as of
no value in the East. A few years ago sturgeon and eel were
not generally eaten. To-day sturgeon is much prized, and in
regions where it was formerly worthless commands a high
price. Many persons have a prejudice against frogs' legs,
while others consider them a great delicacy. In the United
States they are now very commonly eaten, and frog raising for
the market is more or less of an industry. It is doubtful if
Americans ever eat any portion except the legs of frogs, yet in
many regions of Europe the bodies are also used. In Cuba
and other localities squid tentacles are eaten, and are undoubtedly palatable when well prepared. An interesting change of
opinion regarding the use of a sea product may be noted in

the case of abalone, a large mollusk abundant on the California coast, which was formerly disregarded as a food product by Americans, but which, it is said, owing to its use by the Chinese, has become known and is relished.

## CONDITIONS WHICH AFFECT THE MARKET VALUE OF FISH.

The market value of fish is affected by various conditions. Among these are the locality from which they come, the season in which they are taken, and the food on which they have grown. In general, it may be said that fish from clear, cold, or deep water are regarded as preferable to those from shallow or warm water, while fish taken in waters with a rocky or sandy bottom are preferable to those from water with a muddy bottom. Some fish, for instance shad, are at their best during the spawning season, while others should not be eaten during this period. Those fish which feed on small crustacea and the other forms of animal and vegetable life, constituting their natural food, are preferable to those living upon sewage and other matter which may contaminate the waters.

The mode of capture also affects the market value. Fish caught by the gills and allowed to die in the water by slow degrees, as is the case where gill nets are used, undergo decomposition very readily and are inferior for food. Fish are often landed alive and allowed to die slowly. This custom is not only inhumane, but lessens the value of the fish. It has been found that fish killed immediately after catching remain firm and bear shipment better than those allowed to die slowly. The quality of the fish is often injured by improper handling in the fishing boats before placing on the market. Improvements in transportation facilities and in other lines have made it possible to bring fish to market from distant fishing grounds in good condition.

Fresh-water and salt-water fish alike are offered for sale as taken from the water, and preserved in a number of ways. In some cases preservation is only to insure transportation to remote points in good condition. Low temperature is the means most commonly employed for this purpose. By taking advantage of the recent improvements in apparatus and methods of chilling and freezing, fish may be shipped long distances and kept a long time in good condition.

The preservation of meat or fish by methods of cold storage has developed very greatly within recent years and has grown to be a very important industry. The process depends for its success quite largely upon the fact that the activity of microorganisms, which cause putrefactive and other changes in food products, is lessened by cold. In addition to microörganisms, which are almost inevitably present, being found everywhere — in the air, in water, etc. — fish, like other meats, normally contain ferments which cause changes in composition and flavor comparable in some ways with those caused by microorganisms, though they differ in important respects. From recent investigations along these lines, the conclusion was reached that when meat is stored at the freezing point of water (32° F.) the activity of microörganisms is checked, but the action of ferments normally present in the meat still continues, and it ripens, though it does not decay. Such stored meat was regarded as especially suited for roasting or broiling, though not as good as fresh meat for boiling. On the other hand the conclusion was reached that fish cannot be satisfactorily preserved at 32° F., since this temperature is not sufficient to hinder the action of the ferments present in the fish flesh, though it checks the action of microörganisms. The ferments acting upon the tissues in which they occur produce bodies of unpleasant flavor and the fish becomes unpalatable, though it is not in any sense decayed. To successfully hinder the action of the ferments a temperature lower than 32° F. is needed. These facts are in accord with the common practice of shipping fish frozen.

It is stated on good authority that in commercial practice 25° F. is regarded as the proper temperature for storing fish which has been previously frozen. For dried fish the proper temperature is 25° F., for fresh fish 25 to 30° F., for oysters 33 to 40° F., for oysters in the shell 40° F., and for oysters in the tub 35° F. Oysters should not be frozen. It is claimed that oysters may be safely kept for six weeks at a temperature of 40° F., and an instance is recorded in which they were kept ten weeks at this temperature for experimental purposes.

According to the practice of a successful firm dealing in frozen fish, the fish as they are unloaded from the boats are sorted and graded as to size and quality, then placed in galvanized iron pans about 2 feet long, covered with loosely fitting lids, and frozen by keeping them twenty-four hours at a temperature often as low as 16° below zero. The fish are removed from the pans in a solid cake and packed in tiers in the storehouse and marketed frozen. It is said that they may be thus preserved indefinitely, though as a rule frozen fish are only kept six to eight months, being frozen in the spring, when the supply is abundant, and sold in the winter or whenever fresh fish cannot be readily obtained. Such frozen fish are commonly shipped in barrels packed with broken ice in such a manner that the water formed by the melting ice may readily escape.

The flavor of oysters is affected more or less by the locality in which they have grown, those from certain regions being regarded as of very superior quality. The season of the year affects the market value of oysters, although it is noticeable that as methods of transportation and preservation improve, the oyster season becomes longer. This may also be said of lobsters, crabs, etc. Extended investigations, including the conditions affecting the growth and food value of oysters, their parasites and diseases, etc., have been carried on by the New Jersey Experiment Stations. These investigations have shown that oysters rapidly deteriorate when removed from the water, through the fermentative action of bacteria; and that oysters in spawn deteriorate more rapidly than at any other season at the same temperature. However, oysters which are ready to spawn are considered especially palatable if cooked soon after removal from the sea bed.

## PREPARING FISH FOR MARKET.

Fish are sold either " round," *i.e.*, whole, or dressed. Sometimes only the entrails are removed. Often, however, especially when dressed for cooking, the head, fins, and, less frequently, the bones are removed. This entails a considerable loss in weight as well as of nutritive material. It has been assumed that in dressing fish the following percentages are lost: Large-mouthed black bass, sea bass, cisco, kingfish, mullet, white perch, pickerel, pike, tomcod, weakfish, and whitefish, each 17.5 per cent; small-mouthed black bass, eel, Spanish mackerel, porgy, and turbot, each 13.5 per cent; butter-fish, 12.5 per cent; shad, 11 per cent; and brook trout, 16.5 per cent. More recent figures for loss in weight in dressing are as follows: Bullhead, 50 per cent; buffalo-fish and lake sturgeon, 40 per cent; carp and sucker, 35 per cent;

fresh-water sheepshead, 23 per cent; grass pike, black bass, white bass, yellow perch, and salmon, 15 per cent, and eels, 10 per cent.

Large quantities of fish are dried, salted, and smoked, the processes being employed alone or in combination. These methods insure preservation, but at the same time modify the flavor. Several fish products are also prepared by one or more of these processes. Caviar, which may be cited as an example, is usually prepared from sturgeon roe by salting. The methods of salting and packing vary somewhat and give rise to a number of varieties. Although formerly prepared almost exclusively in Russia, caviar is now made to a large extent in the United States. In methods of drying fish the Chinese are very expert, producing, among other goods, dried oysters, which are said to be palatable and of good quality. Dried fish and fish products are also important in the diet of the Japanese.

When fish are salted and cured there is a considerable loss in weight, due to removal of the entrails, drying, etc. Cod-fish lose 60 per cent in preparation for market. If the market-dried fish is boned there is a further loss of 20 per cent. The loss in weight of pollock from the round to the market-dried fish is 60 per cent; haddock, 62 per cent; hake, 56 per cent; and cusk, 51 per cent.

The Scandinavians make a number of fish products in which the fish is allowed to ferment, the methods followed being in a way comparable with those employed in the manufacture of sauerkraut. In Java the natives are very partial to fish which has undergone fermentation, sometimes apparently putrefactive and resulting in a product which would be considered entirely unfit for food from a western standpoint.

The canning industry has been enormously developed in recent years and thousands of pounds of fish, oysters, lobsters, etc., are annually preserved in this way. In canning, the fish or other material is heated (the air being sometimes exhausted also) to destroy microörganisms, and sealed to prevent access of air, which would introduce microörganisms as well as oxygen. Thus the canned material is preserved from oxidation and decomposition. The processes of canning have been much improved, so that the original flavor is largely retained, while the goods may be kept for an indefinite period. Fish, as well as meat, is usually canned in its own juice or cooked in some form, though sardines and some other fishes are commonly preserved in oil.

Various kinds of fish extract, clam juice, etc., are offered for sale. These are similar in form to meat extract. There are also a number of fish pastes and similar products — anchovy paste, for instance — which are used as relishes or condiments.

Preservatives such as salicylate of soda are employed to some extent in marketing fish and especially oysters. The extended use of such materials is not desirable since some of them are justly regarded as harmful.

Oysters and other shellfish are placed on the market alive in the shell or are removed from the shell and kept in good condition by chilling or other means. Oysters in the shell are usually transported in barrels or sacks. Shipment is made to far inland points in refrigerator cars and to Europe in the cold-storage chambers of vessels. Large quantities of shellfish are also canned. Oysters are often sold as they are taken from the salt water. However, the practice of " freshening," " fattening," or " floating " is very widespread — that is, oysters are placed in fresh or brackish water for a short period. They become plump in appearance and have a different flavor from those taken directly from salt water. As noted, care should be taken that the oysters are grown and fattened in water which is not contaminated by sewage.

Lobsters, crabs, and other crustacea are usually sold alive. Sometimes they are boiled before they are placed on the market. Large quantities of lobsters, shrimps, and crabs are canned.

Turtle and terrapin are usually marketed alive. Turtle soup, however, is canned in large quantities. Frogs are marketed alive or dressed, and may be eaten at all seasons, but are in the best condition in the fall or winter. It is said that Minnesota is the center of the frog industry in the United States, the catch for a year being about 5,000,000 frogs, or not far from 500,000 dozen pairs of frogs' legs, the annual value of the frog business being upward of $100,000.

# NUTRITIVE VALUE OF FISH.

## COMPOSITION OF FISH.

Fish contain the same kinds of nutrients as other food materials. In general it may be said that food (fish, meat, cereals, vegetables, etc.) serves a two-fold purpose : It supplies the body with material for building and repairing its tissues and fluids, and furnishes it with fuel for maintaining body temperature and for supplying the energy necessary for muscular work.

In a way the body is like a machine, with food for its source of motive power. The body differs from a machine, however, in that the fuel, *i.e.*, food, is used to build it as well as supply it with energy. Further, if the body is supplied with more food than is needed, the excess can be stored as reserve material, usually in the form of fat. In the furnace, fuel is burned quickly, yielding heat and certain chemical products — carbon dioxid, water vapor, and nitrogen. In the body the combustion takes place much more slowly, but in general the final products are the same. The combustion of nitrogen is, however, not so complete as in a furnace. Due allowance is made for this fact in calculations involving the question of the energy which food will furnish.

Food consists of an edible portion and refuse, *i.e.*, bones of fish and meat, shells of oysters, bran of wheat, etc. Although foods are so different in appearance, chemical analysis shows that they are all made up of a comparatively small number of chemical compounds. These are water and the so-called nutrients, protein or nitrogenous materials, fat, carbohydrates, and ash or mineral matter. Familiar examples of protein are lean of fish and meat, white of egg, casein of milk (and cheese), and gluten of wheat. Fat is found in fat fish and meat, in lard, fat of milk (butter), and oils, such as olive oil. Starches, sugars, and woody fiber or cellulose form the bulk of the carbohydrates. Certain carbohydrates are found in meat and fish, although the amount is not large. The protein, fats, and carbohydrates are all organic substances — that is, they can be burned with the formation of various gases, chiefly carbon dioxid and water, leaving no solid residue. The mineral matters will not burn, and are left behind when organic matter is ignited. By analysis the nutrients have been found to be made up of a comparatively small number of chemical elements in varying combinations. These are nitrogen, carbon, oxygen, hydrogen, phosphorus, sulphur, calcium, magnesium, sodium, potassium, silicon, chlorin, fluorin, and iron. Doubtless no single nutrient contains all these elements. The body tissues and fluids contain nitrogen; and hence protein, which alone supplies nitrogen to the body, is a necessary factor in food. All the nutrients except mineral matter contain carbon, oxygen, and hydrogen, and can supply them to the body. Protein, fat, and carbohydrates are all sources of energy.

The value of a food as a source of material for building and repairing the body is shown by its chemical composition — that is, by the amount of digestible nutrients which it contains. Some other means are necessary to show its value as a source of energy. It is known that all energy may be measured in terms of heat. In order to have some measure for expressing the amount of heat the calorie is taken as a unit. Roughly speaking, this is the amount of heat required to raise the temperature of 1 pound of water 4° F. One pound of starch would, if burned and all the heat utilized, raise 1,900 pounds of water 4° in temperature; or it would raise 5 gallons of water from the freezing point to the boiling point, but would not cause it to boil.

The number of calories which different foods will supply may be determined by burning them in an apparatus called a calorimeter, or by taking the sum of the calories which it is calculated the protein, fat, and carbohydrates making up the food would furnish. It has been found by experiment that the fuel value of a pound of protein as ordinarily burned in the body is 1,860 calories; the fuel value of a pound of carbohydrates is the same, while that of a pound of fat is 2.25 times as great.

The value of a food is usually judged by several different standards. Thus it must be digestible and palatable, furnish the nutrients needed by the system in proper amounts, and be reasonably cheap.

The relative nutritive value of any food may be learned by comparing its composition and energy value with similar data for other foods. Table 1 shows the composition of a number of food fishes, fresh and preserved in a variety of ways; oysters, clams, and other mollusks; lobsters, shrimps, crawfish, and crabs; turtle and terrapin, and frogs' legs. For purposes of comparison the analyses of a number of kinds of meat, vegetables, and other common food materials, are included.

In several cases the analysis of fish, whole and dressed, is given. Usually the composition of the dressed fish was computed from that of whole fish with the aid of the figures for loss of weight in dressing for market, mentioned on page 6.

TABLE I. — Composition of fish, mollusks, crustaceans, etc.

| Kind of Food Material. | Refuse (Bone, Skin, etc.). | Salt. | Water. | Protein by Factor (N×6.25). | Fat. | Carbohydrates. | Ash or Mineral Matter. | Total Nutrients. | Fuel Value per Pound. |
|---|---|---|---|---|---|---|---|---|---|
| | Per ct. | Per ct. | Per ct. | Per ct. | Per ct. | Per ct. | Per ct. | Per ct. | Calories. |
| **FRESH FISH.** | | | | | | | | | |
| Alewife, whole | 49.5 | ........ | 37.6 | 9.8 | 2.4 | ........ | 0.8 | 13.0 | 277 |
| Bass, large-mouthed black, dressed | 46.7 | ........ | 41.9 | 10.3 | .5 | ........ | .6 | 11.4 | 209 |
| Bass, large-mouthed black, whole | 56.0 | ........ | 34.6 | 8.5 | .4 | ........ | .5 | 9.4 | 172 |
| Bass, small-mouthed black, dressed | 46.4 | ........ | 40.1 | 11.7 | 1.3 | ........ | .7 | 13.7 | 263 |
| Bass, small-mouthed black, whole | 53.6 | ........ | 34.7 | 10.1 | 1.1 | ........ | .6 | 11.8 | 227 |
| Bass, sea, dressed | 46.8 | ........ | 42.2 | 10.5 | .2 | ........ | .7 | 11.4 | 200 |
| Bass, sea, whole | 56.1 | ........ | 34.8 | 8.7 | .2 | ........ | .6 | 9.5 | 168 |
| Bass, striped, dressed | 51.2 | ........ | 37.4 | 8.8 | 2.2 | ........ | .5 | 11.5 | 249 |
| Blackfish, dressed | 55.7 | ........ | 35.0 | 8.4 | .5 | ........ | .5 | 9.4 | 172 |
| Bluefish, dressed | 48.6 | ........ | 40.3 | 10.0 | .6 | ........ | .7 | 11.3 | 204 |
| Butterfish, dressed | 34.6 | ........ | 45.8 | 11.8 | 7.2 | ........ | .7 | 19.7 | 503 |
| Butterfish, whole | 42.8 | ........ | 40.1 | 10.3 | 6.3 | ........ | .6 | 17.2 | 440 |
| Carp (European analysis) | 37.1 | ........ | 48.4 | ........ | .7 | ........ | .9 | 14.5 | 263 |
| Cod, dressed | 29.9 | ........ | 58.5 | 11.1 | .2 | ........ | .8 | 12.1 | 209 |
| Cod, steaks | 9.2 | ........ | 72.4 | 17.0 | .5 | ........ | 1.0 | 18.5 | 327 |
| Cusk, dressed | 40.3 | ........ | 49.0 | 10.1 | .1 | ........ | .5 | 10.7 | 186 |
| Eel, salt-water, dressed | 20.2 | ........ | 57.2 | 14.8 | 7.2 | ........ | .8 | 22.8 | 558 |
| Flounder, common, dressed | 57.0 | ........ | 35.8 | 6.4 | .3 | ........ | .6 | 7.3 | 127 |
| Flounder, winter, dressed | 56.2 | ........ | 37.0 | 6.3 | .2 | ........ | .5 | 7.0 | 122 |

| | | | | | | | | | |
|---|---|---|---|---|---|---|---|---|---|
| Hake, dressed | 52.2 | | 39.5 | 7.3 | .3 | | .5 | 8.1 | 145 |
| Haddock, dressed | 51.0 | | 40.0 | 8.4 | .2 | | .6 | 9.2 | 159 |
| Halibut, dressed | 17.7 | | 61.9 | 15.3 | 4.4 | | .9 | 20.6 | 454 |
| Herring, whole | 42.6 | | 41.7 | 11.2 | 3.9 | | .9 | 16.0 | 363 |
| Mackerel, dressed | 40.7 | | 43.7 | 11.6 | 3.5 | | .7 | 15.8 | 354 |
| Mackerel, Spanish, dressed | 24.4 | | 51.4 | 16.3 | 7.2 | | 1.2 | 24.7 | 585 |
| Mackerel, Spanish, whole | 34.6 | | 44.5 | 14.1 | 6.2 | | 1.0 | 21.3 | 508 |
| Mullet, dressed | 49.0 | | 38.2 | 9.9 | 2.4 | | .6 | 12.9 | 277 |
| Mullet, whole | 57.9 | | 31.5 | 8.2 | 2.0 | | .5 | 8.9 | 231 |
| Perch, white, dressed | 54.6 | | 34.4 | 8.8 | 1.8 | | .5 | 11.1 | 231 |
| Perch, white, whole | 62.5 | | 28.4 | 7.3 | 1.5 | | .4 | 9.2 | 195 |
| Perch, yellow, dressed | 35.1 | | 50.7 | 12.8 | .7 | | .9 | 14.4 | 259 |
| Pickerel, dressed | 35.9 | | 51.2 | 12.0 | .2 | | .7 | 12.9 | 227 |
| Pickerel, whole | 47.1 | | 42.2 | 9.9 | .2 | | .6 | 10.7 | 186 |
| Pollock, dressed | 28.5 | | 54.3 | 15.4 | .6 | | 1.1 | 17.1 | 304 |
| Pompano, whole | 45.5 | | 39.5 | 10.3 | 4.3 | | .5 | 15.1 | 358 |
| Porgy, dressed | 53.7 | | 34.6 | 8.6 | 2.4 | | .7 | 11.7 | 254 |
| Porgy, whole | 60.0 | | 29.9 | 7.4 | 2.1 | | .6 | 10.1 | 218 |
| Red grouper, dressed | 55.9 | | 35.0 | 8.5 | .2 | | .5 | 9.2 | 163 |
| Red snapper, dressed | 45.3 | | 43.7 | 10.6 | .3 | | .7 | 11.6 | 204 |
| Salmon, California (sections) | 10.3 | | 57.9 | 16.7 | 14.8 | | .9 | 32.4 | 903 |
| Salmon, Maine, dressed | 23.8 | | 51.2 | 15.0 | 9.5 | | .9 | 25.4 | 658 |
| Shad, dressed | 43.9 | | 39.6 | 10.6 | 5.4 | | .8 | 16.8 | 408 |
| Shad, whole | 50.1 | | 35.2 | 9.4 | 4.8 | | .7 | 14.9 | 363 |
| Shad, roe | | | 71.2 | 23.5 | 3.8 | | 1.5 | 28.8 | 581 |
| Smelt, whole | 41.9 | | 46.1 | 10.1 | 1.0 | | 1.0 | 12.1 | 222 |
| Sturgeon, dressed | 14.4 | | 67.4 | 15.1 | 1.6 | | 1.2 | 17.9 | 340 |
| Tomcod, dressed | 51.4 | | 39.6 | 8.4 | .3 | | .5 | 9.2 | 163 |
| Tomcod, whole | 59.9 | | 32.7 | 6.9 | .2 | | .4 | 7.5 | 132 |
| Trout, brook, dressed | 37.9 | | 48.4 | 11.9 | 1.3 | | .7 | 13.9 | 268 |
| Trout, brook, whole | 48.1 | | 40.4 | 9.9 | 1.1 | | .6 | 11.6 | 222 |
| Trout, lake, dressed | 37.5 | | 44.4 | 11.0 | 6.2 | | .7 | 17.9 | 449 |
| Turbot, dressed | 39.5 | | 43.1 | 8.9 | 8.7 | | .8 | 18.4 | 513 |

TABLE I. — Composition of fish, mollusks, crustaceans, etc. — Continued.

| Kind of Food Material. | Refuse (Bone, Skin, etc.). | Salt. | Water. | Protein by Factor (N×6.25). | Fat. | Carbohydrates. | Ash or Mineral Matter. | Total Nutrients. | Fuel Value per Pound. |
|---|---|---|---|---|---|---|---|---|---|
| | Per ct. | Per ct. | Per ct. | Per ct. | Per ct. | Per ct. | Per ct. | Per ct. | Calories. |
| **FRESH FISH — Cont.** | | | | | | | | | |
| Turbot, whole | 47.7 | ..... | 37.3 | 7.7 | 7.5 | ..... | .7 | 15.9 | 445 |
| Weakfish, dressed | 41.7 | ..... | 46.1 | 10.4 | 1.3 | ..... | .7 | 12.4 | 240 |
| Weakfish, whole | 51.9 | ..... | 38.0 | 8.6 | 1.1 | ..... | .6 | 10.3 | 200 |
| Whitefish, dressed | 43.6 | ..... | 39.4 | 12.8 | 3.6 | ..... | .9 | 17.3 | 376 |
| Whitefish, whole | 53.5 | ..... | 32.5 | 10.6 | 3.0 | ..... | .7 | 14.3 | 313 |
| General average of fresh fish as sold | 41.6 | ..... | 44.6 | 10.9 | 2.4 | ..... | .7 | 14.0 | 295 |
| **PRESERVED FISH.** | | | | | | | | | |
| Mackerel, No. 1, salted | 19.7 | 8.3 | 34.8 | 13.9 | 21.2 | ..... | 2.1 | 37.2 | 1,107 |
| Cod, salted and dried | 24.9 | 17.3 | 40.2 | 19.0 | 4 | ..... | 1.2 | 20.6 | 363 |
| Cod, boneless codfish, salted and dried | ..... | 21.5 | 54.4 | 26.3 | .3 | ..... | 1.7 | 28.3 | 490 |
| Caviar | ..... | ..... | 38.1 | 30.0 | 19.7 | 7.6 | *4.6 | 61.9 | 1,479 |
| Herring, salted, smoked, and dried | 44.4 | 6.5 | 19.2 | 20.5 | 8.8 | ..... | .9 | 30.2 | 726 |
| Haddock, salted, smoked, and dried | 32.2 | 1.4 | 49.2 | 15.8 | .1 | ..... | 1.0 | 16.9 | 290 |
| Halibut, salted, smoked, and dried | 7.0 | 12.0 | 46.0 | 19.3 | 14.0 | ..... | 1.9 | 35.2 | 916 |
| Sardines, canned | 5.0 | ..... | 53.6 | 23.7 | 12.1 | ..... | 5.3 | 41.1 | 916 |
| Salmon, canned | 14.2 | ..... | 56.8 | 19.5 | 7.5 | ..... | *2.0 | 29.0 | 658 |

|  |  |  |  |  |  |  |  |  |  |
|---|---|---|---|---|---|---|---|---|---|
| Mackerel, canned |  | 1.9 | 68.2 | 19.6 | 8.7 |  | 1.3 | 29.6 | 708 |
| Mackerel, salt, canned | 19.7 | 8.3 | 34.8 | 13.9 | 21.2 |  | 2.1 | 37.2 | 1,107 |
| Tunny, canned |  |  | 72.7 | 21.7 | 4.1 |  | 1.7 | 27.5 | 558 |
| Haddock, smoked, cooked, canned |  | 5.6 | 68.7 | 22.3 | 2.3 |  | 1.6 | 26.2 | 499 |
| **MOLLUSKS.** |  |  |  |  |  |  |  |  |  |
| Oysters, solids |  |  | 83.3 | 6.0 | 1.3 | 3.3 | 1.1 | 11.7 | 222 |
| Oysters, in shell | 81.4 |  | 16.1 | 1.2 | .2 | .7 | .4 | 2.5 | 41 |
| Oysters, canned |  |  | 83.4 | 8.8 | 2.4 | 3.9 | 1.5 | 16.6 | 327 |
| Scallops |  |  | 80.3 | 14.8 | .1 | 3.4 | 1.4 | 19.7 | 336 |
| Long clams, in shell | 41.9 |  | 49.9 | 5.0 | .6 | 1.1 | 1.5 | 8.2 | 136 |
| Long clams, canned |  |  | 84.5 | 9.0 | 1.3 | 2.9 | 2.3 | 15.5 | 268 |
| Round clams, removed from shell |  |  | 80.8 | 10.6 | 1.1 | 5.2 | 2.3 | 19.2 | 331 |
| Round clams, in shell | 67.5 |  | 28.0 | 2.1 | .1 | 1.4 | .9 | 4.5 | 68 |
| Round clams, canned |  |  | 82.9 | 10.5 | .8 | 3.0 | 2.8 | 17.1 | 277 |
| Mussels | 46.7 |  | 44.9 | 4.6 | .6 | 2.2 | 1.0 | 8.4 | 150 |
| General average of mollusks (exclusive of canned) | 59.4 |  | 34.7 | 3.2 | .4 | 1.4 | .9 | 5.9 | 99 |
| **CRUSTACEANS.** |  |  |  |  |  |  |  |  |  |
| Lobster, in shell | 61.7 |  | 30.7 | 5.9 | .7 | .2 | .8 | 7.6 | 141 |
| Lobster, canned |  |  | 77.8 | 18.1 | 1.1 | .5 | 2.5 | 22.2 | 381 |
| Crawfish, in shell | 86.6 |  | 10.9 | 2.1 | .1 | .1 | .2 | 2.5 | 45 |
| Crabs, in shell | 52.4 |  | 36.7 | 7.9 | .9 | .6 | 1.5 | 10.9 | 191 |
| Crabs, canned |  |  | 80.0 | 15.8 | 1.5 | .7 | 2.0 | 20.0 | 358 |
| Shrimp, canned |  |  | 70.8 | 25.4 | 1.0 | .2 | 2.6 | 29.2 | 503 |
| Fresh abalone |  |  | 72.8 | 22.2 | .3 | 3.3 | 1.4 | 27.2 | 501 |
| Canned abalone, flesh |  |  | 73.2 | 21.7 | .1 | 3.7 | 1.3 | 26.8 | 489 |
| Canned abalone, liquid in can |  |  | 93.8 | 4.4 | .1 | .2 | 1.5 | 6.2 | 93 |
| Dried abalone |  |  | 39.7 | 36.0 | .5 | 20.9 | 2.9 | 60.3 | 1,079 |
| General average of crustaceans (exclusive of canned and dried) | 50.2 |  | 37.8 | 9.5 | .5 | 1.0 | 1.0 | 12.0 | 220 |

\* Including salt.

TABLE I. — *Composition of fish, mollusks, crustaceans, etc.* — Concluded.

| Kind of Food Material. | Refuse (Bone, Skin, etc.). | Salt. | Water. | Protein by Factor (N×6.25). | Fat. | Carbohydrates. | Ash or Mineral Matter. | Total Nutrients. | Fuel Value per Pound. |
|---|---|---|---|---|---|---|---|---|---|
| | Per ct. | Per ct. | Per ct. | Per ct. | Per ct. | Per ct. | Per ct. | Per ct. | Calories. |
| **TERRAPIN, TURTLE, ETC.** | | | | | | | | | |
| Terrapin, in shell | 75.4 | ...... | 18.3 | 5.2 | .9 | ........ | .2 | 6.3 | 132 |
| Green turtle, in shell | 76.0 | ...... | 19.2 | 4.7 | .1 | ........ | .3 | 5.1 | 91 |
| Average of turtle and terrapin | 75.6 | ...... | 18.8 | 4.9 | .5 | ........ | .3 | 5.7 | 111 |
| Frogs' legs | 32.0 | ...... | 56.9 | 10.5 | .1 | ........ | .7 | 11.3 | 195 |
| General average of fish, mollusks, crustaceans, etc. | 45.0 | ...... | 42.3 | 9.7 | 2.1 | .2 | .7 | 12.7 | 264 |
| **OTHER ANIMAL FOODS.** | | | | | | | | | |
| Beef, side, medium fat | 17.4 | ...... | 49.4 | 14.8 | 18.1 | ........ | .7 | 33.6 | 998 |
| Veal, side | 22.6 | ...... | 55.2 | 15.6 | 6.3 | ........ | .8 | 22.7 | 535 |
| Mutton, side | 19.3 | ...... | 43.3 | 13.0 | 24.0 | ........ | .7 | 37.7 | 1,207 |
| Average of beef, veal, and mutton | 19.4 | ...... | 49.3 | 14.5 | 16.1 | ........ | .7 | 31.3 | 913 |
| Pork, side | 11.2 | ...... | 26.1 | 8.3 | 54.8 | ........ | .4 | 63.5 | 2,363 |
| Chicken | 25.9 | ...... | 47.1 | 13.7 | 12.3 | ........ | .7 | 26.7 | 744 |
| Turkey | 22.7 | ...... | 42.4 | 16.1 | 18.4 | ........ | .8 | 35.3 | 1,034 |
| Milk | ...... | ...... | 87.0 | 3.3 | 4.0 | 5.0 | .7 | 13.0 | 313 |
| **VEGETABLE FOODS.** | | | | | | | | | |
| Wheat flour | ...... | ...... | 12.0 | 11.4 | 1.0 | 75.1 | .5 | 88.0 | 1,610 |
| Corn meal | ...... | ...... | 12.5 | 9.2 | 1.9 | 75.4 | 1.0 | 87.5 | 1,610 |
| Wheat bread (from patent flour) | ...... | ...... | 35.3 | 9.2 | 1.3 | 53.1 | 1.1 | 64.7 | 1,215 |

| | | | | | | | |
|---|---|---|---|---|---|---|---|
| Beans, dried | ...... | 12.6 | 22.5 | 1.8 | 59.6 | 3.5 | 87.4 | 1,560 |
| Potato | 20.0 | 62.6 | 1.8 | .1 | 14.7 | .8 | 17.4 | 303 |
| Cabbage | 15.0 | 77.7 | 1.4 | .2 | 4.8 | .9 | 7.3 | 122 |
| Corn, canned | ...... | 76.1 | 2.8 | 1.2 | 19.0 | .9 | 23.9 | 445 |
| Salad greens | ...... | 86.7 | 4.2 | .6 | 6.3 | 2.2 | 13.3 | 213 |
| Apples | 25.0 | 63.3 | .3 | .3 | 10.8 | .3 | 11.7 | 213 |
| Bananas | 35.0 | 48.9 | .8 | .4 | 14.3 | .6 | 16.1 | 290 |
| Strawberries | 5.0 | 85.9 | .9 | .6 | 7.0 | .6 | 9.1 | 168 |
| Sugar | ...... | ...... | ...... | ...... | 100.0 | ...... | 100.0 | 1,860 |

The above list includes the more important food fishes, water invertebrates, etc.  There are numbers of other fish which are eaten to a greater or less extent.  In general it may be said their composition would be similar to that of the fishes included in the table.

In a number of cases cited in the table above more than one specimen was analyzed, although only the averages are given in the table.  In such cases the samples showed more or less variation in total nutrients, but the variation was due more especially to the fats.  Thus the fat in the flesh of seven specimens of shad ranged from 6.5 to 13.6 per cent; in fresh mackerel from 2.2 to 16.3 per cent, and in fresh halibut from 2.2 to 10.6 per cent.  The protein and ash or mineral matter remained practically the same in all the specimens where the wide fat variation was noticeable, an increase of fat being accompanied by a decrease of water.

An extended study of the chemical composition of fish was recently carried on at the zoölogical station at Naples by Lichtenfelt.  It was found that the composition of the muscular tissue changes periodically with age, nutrition, and reproduction.  Under the influence of hunger the amount of water in the flesh is increased and the proportion of solids diminished.  The richer the muscles in fat, the greater the loss as compared with lean fish.  The amount of protein is also diminished not only in salmon, but in other sorts of fish.  The amount of insoluble proteids is decreased while the proportion of soluble proteids may be either increased or lowered according to circumstances.  Muscular activity in connection with hunger seems a condition especially suited to induce an increase of soluble proteids in fish flesh.

It will be seen from the table that fish is essentially a nitrogenous food.  In this it resembles meat.  Neither fish nor meat is a source of carbohydrates.  Oysters and other shellfish contain some carbohydrates, but the foods which supply this group of nutrients most abundantly are sugar and the cereal grains.  The place of fish in the diet, if judged by its composition, is therefore the same as that of meat — that is, it supplements cereals and other vegetables, the most of which, as wheat, rye, maize, rice, potatoes, etc., are deficient in protein, the chief nutrient in the flesh of fish.  As regards the relative nutritive value of meat and fish, Atwater's conclusion, from a large number of investigations, was that the only considerable difference is in the proportion of water and fat present, the flesh of the fish having water where meat has fat.

From the standpoint of both nutritive value and palatability fish, according to a recent German investigator, is an important food product and, as shown by his experiments, equal to beef as a source of energy in the diet. It produces the same sensation of satiety and this persists for as long a time. It was found that fish caused the excretion of a smaller amount of uric acid than meat.

In general, it may be said that fish, meat, eggs, milk, etc., also cereals and vegetable foods, all supply fat, the amount varying in the different materials. Fish usually contains less fat than is found in meat. There is, however, much difference in the fat content of the various kinds of fish. They may, indeed, be roughly divided into three classes: The first class would include those containing over 5 per cent fat; the second, those containing between 2 and 5 per cent, and the third, those containing less than 2 per cent. The first group would include such fish as salmon, shad, herring, Spanish mackerel, and butter-fish; the second, whitefish, mackerel, mullet, halibut, and porgy; the third, smelt, black bass, blue-fish, white perch, weakfish, brook trout, hake, flounder, yellow perch, pike, pickerel, sea bass, cod, and haddock.

As regards nitrogenous constituents, fish flesh contains more gelatin-yielding material (collagen) and less extractive material (meat bases) than meat. As is well known, the characteristic red color of blood and muscular tissue is due to the presence of a substance called hemoglobin. The flesh and blood of fish contain less of this and allied coloring matters than meat, which accounts for the light color commonly observed in fish flesh. The flesh of some fishes, like salmon, has a decided color. It is not due, however, to hemoglobin, but to the presence of a special pigment.

The so-called nitrogenous extractives ("meat extract"), contained in small quantities in fish as in other animal foods, are doubtless useful in nutrition, although opinions have differed as to their real function. Recent investigations indicate very strongly that flesh extractives play an important part in stomach digestion, as they have been shown to induce an abundant flow of normal gastric juice. Many of the ordinary food materials possess this property also, but the flesh extractives seem to be especially suited to the purpose. They do not, it is true, furnish the body much food material, but they are nevertheless important if they normally help it to digest other foods.

With the exception of a few kinds which are preserved whole, preserved fish, as a rule, show a small percentage of refuse. The percentage of actual nutrients is much larger than in the corresponding fresh fish, owing to the removal of a large part of the refuse and more or less water. The gain in nutrients is mostly represented by protein, which is the most valuable nutrient.

Dried fish is richer in nutritive material, pound for pound, than fresh fish, since it has been concentrated by evaporation. It has been found that the average loss in weight in drying is about 30 per cent, or less than the average values for different kinds of meat. The loss in weight is chiefly due to the evaporation of water, though in some cases dried fish contains a little less ether extract than fresh fish.

When foods are cooked there is, generally speaking, a loss of weight owing to the evaporation of water, and in the ordinary methods of cooking fish and meat some nutritive material is lost also. In recent experiments it was found that the water in which fish was boiled contained 9 to 11 per cent of the total fish protein.

Canned fish, which is in effect cooked fish, compares favorably as regards composition with the fresh material. Generally speaking, the amount of refuse is small, since the portions commonly rejected in preparation for the table have been removed before canning.

The various kinds of shellfish resemble meat and food fishes in general composition. They contain, however, an appreciable amount of carbohydrates. Oysters are the most important of the shellfish, judging by the relative amount consumed. Speaking roughly, a quart of oysters contains on an average about the same quantity of actual nutritive substance as a quart of milk, or three-fourths of a pound of beef, or 2 pounds of fresh codfish, or a pound of bread; but, while the weight of actual nutriment in the different quantities of food materials named is very nearly the same, the kind is widely different. That of the lean meat or codfish consists mostly of protein, the substance whose principal function is to make or repair blood, muscle, tendon, bone, brain, and other nitrogenous tissues. That of bread contains considerable protein, but a much larger proportion of starch, with a little fat and other compounds which supply the body with heat and muscular power. The nutritive substance of oysters contains considerable protein and energy-yielding ingredients. Oysters come nearer to milk than almost any other common food material as regards both the amounts and the relative proportions of nutrients.

Apparently as the oyster grows older, at least up to a certain time, not only do the proportions of flesh and liquids increase more rapidly than the shells, but the proportion of nutrients in the edible portion increases also; that is to say, 100 pounds of young oysters in the shell appear to contain less of flesh and of liquids than 100 pounds of older ones, and when both have been shucked a pound of shell contents from the older oysters would contain more nutriment than a pound from the younger.

Considering the edible portion of the oyster, after it has been removed from the shell, the differences in different specimens are much greater than is commonly supposed. This is apparent when a comparison is made of either the flesh (meat) or liquids (liquor) of different specimens, or the whole edible portion, the meat (solids) and liquor together. The percentage of water in the edible portion of different specimens of oysters which were analyzed in experiments conducted for the United States Fish Commission varied from about 83.4 to 91.4 per cent, and averaged 87.3 per cent. This makes the amounts of "water-free substance," *i.e.*, actually nutritive ingredients, vary from 16.6 to 8.6 and average 12.7 per cent of the whole weight of the edible portion (shell contents) of the animals. In other words, the nutritive material in a quart (about 2 pounds) of shell contents (solids) varied from 2.75 to 5.33 ounces.

With oysters, long clams, and round clams in the shell there is naturally a large percentage of waste, as the shell constitutes a large proportion of the total weight. The average of 34 specimens of oysters in the shell, for instance, shows only 2.3 per cent of actual nutrients. Clams and mussels show a somewhat higher percentage.

Where these various shellfish are purchased as "solids" — that is, removed from the shell — a comparatively high price is usually paid. Where they are purchased in the shell, there is a very large percentage of waste. The conclusion is therefore warranted that, from a pecuniary standpoint, they are not the most economical of foods for the consumer. On the other hand, they have a useful place in the diet in helping to supply the variety which is apparently needed to insure the best workings of the digestive system. Often flavor has a value which cannot be estimated in dollars and cents.

It does not seem probable that the oysters would secure food enough to make appreciable gain in weight in the short time in which they remain in the fresh or brackish water.

It is known that when a solution of salts is separated by a suitable membrane from water containing a lesser quantity of salts in solution that the passage of salts immediately begins from the concentrated to the dilute solution. This is practically the condition which exists when the oyster is transferred from salt to fresh or brackish water. The fleshy portions of the body which are inclosed in a membrane contain salts in solution. As long as the oyster stays in salt water the solution of salts within its body would naturally be in equilibrium with the water outside. When the oyster is brought into fresh or brackish water, *i.e.*, into a more dilute solution, it might be expected that the salts in the more concentrated solution within the body would pass out and a larger amount of fresh water enter and produce such a distention as actually takes place during floating. Careful experiments have shown that this supposition is entirely correct — that is, the oysters actually gain in weight. This is due largely to the fact that they lose mineral matter and gain a considerable amount of water. At the same time there is a slight loss of nutrients. When in their natural condition oysters contain from one-eighth to one-fifth more nutritive material than when fattened. In the opinion of very many consumers the improvement in appearance and flavor due to the removal of the salts more than compensates for the loss in nutritive value. It seems also to be a matter of common opinion that oysters keep better when part of the salts has been removed by " floating." However, the experiments of the New Jersey Experiment Stations have shown that freshened oysters will not remain alive as long as those taken directly from salt water. Freshening increases very rapidly the rate of weakening and decay (the life period being reduced one-half).

Frequently oysters become more or less green in color There is a widespread opinion that " greening " is injurious. The color has been attributed to disease, to parasites, and to the presence of copper.

Experiments have shown that quite commonly the green color of American oysters at least is due to the fact that they have fed on green plants of very simple structure which are sometimes found to be abundant in salt or brackish waters. The green coloring matter of the plants is dissolved by the oyster juices and colors the tissues. The opinion of those who have investigated the matter carefully is that such green color is harmless. It may be removed, if desired, by placing the live oysters for a time in water where the green plants are not abundant. In Europe similar green oysters, called " groenbarden" or " Marennes," are especially prized, and to meet the demand oysters are greened by placing them as soon as captured in sea water, where they are kept for months and fed on a species of seaweed which imparts the coloring matter to the gills.

From carefully conducted investigations it appears that in some cases green oysters owe their color to the presence of copper. Such oysters are not generally considered wholesome. Green oysters containing copper differ in appearance from those owing their green tint to vegetable coloring matter, being grass green and not dark green in color and having a verdigris-like slimy secretion on the folds of the mantle. It is said that after the addition of vinegar a steel fork stuck into such oysters becomes coated with copper and that if ammonia is added the oysters become dark blue.

As will be seen by the figures in Table 1, fresh and canned abalone correspond quite closely to oyster and clam products similarly prepared. As shown by some tests carried on by Jaffa and Mendel, abalone flesh is especially rich in glycogen. This fact is also emphasized by the figures in the table above, especially those for dried abalone, which are quoted from unpublished analyses made by Jaffa at the California Experiment Station. Generally speaking, compared with other sea products, the abalone is a nutritious food. Its flavor is said, by those who are familiar with it, to be excellent. Large quantities of abalone are canned, the flesh being cut into pieces of suitable size. Abalone is also dried extensively, the canned and the dried products finding a ready market among the Chinese.

Lobsters, crabs, shrimps, and crawfish are shown by analysis to contain a fairly large percentage of nutrients, as is especially noticeable when the composition of the flesh alone is considered. They resemble the lean rather than the fat fish in composition. Lobsters and crabs are very much alike as regards the structure of the flesh, which in each case consists of coarse dense-walled fibers. Lobsters and similar foods are prized for their delicate flavor. Except in certain regions where they are very abundant and the cost correspondingly low, they must be regarded as delicacies rather than as staple articles of diet. This is, however, a condition entirely apart from their composition. Judged by this alone, they are valuable foods, and may profitably be employed to give variety to the diet.

Although the total amount of turtle and terrapin used in the United States is quite large, the quantity is small as compared with the consumption of such foods as fish proper and oysters. As shown by their composition, turtle and terrapin are nutritious foods, although, under existing conditions, they are expensive delicacies rather than staple and economical articles of diet.

The total amount of frogs consumed per year for food is considerable. As shown by analysis, frogs' legs contain a fairly high percentage of protein. Only the hind legs are commonly eaten. The meat on other portions of the body is edible, although the amount is small, and is eaten in some localities. The prejudice which formerly existed against frogs' legs as a food was doubtless based on their appearance or some similar reason, as they are known to be wholesome.

## COST OF PROTEIN AND ENERGY IN FISH AND OTHER FOOD MATERIALS.

As previously stated, the two functions of food are to furnish protein for building and repairing the body and to supply energy for heat and muscular work. Although fish and meats in general may be regarded as sources of protein, they nevertheless furnish considerable energy. Indeed, those containing an abundance of fat supply a large amount of energy — that is, have a high fuel value. If a food contains little protein or energy and is high in price, it is evident that it is really expensive. On the other hand, a food may be high in price but in reality be cheap, if it furnishes a large amount of protein or energy or both. Foods which supply an abundance of protein or energy or both at a reasonable price are evidently of the greatest importance from the standpoint of economy.

In Table 2 is shown how much a pound of protein, or 1,000 calories of energy, would cost when supplied by a number of kinds of fish and other foods at certain prices, and also the amount of total food, protein, and energy which 10 cents' worth of the fish and other food materials would furnish.

TABLE 2. — *Comparative cost of protein and energy as furnished by a number of food materials, at certain prices.*

| Kind of Food Material. | Price per Pound. | Cost of 1 Pound Protein. | Cost of 1,000 Calories Energy. | Amounts for 10 Cents. | | |
|---|---|---|---|---|---|---|
| | | | | Total Weight of Food Material. | Protein. | Energy. |
| | *Cents.* | *Dollars.* | *Cents.* | *Pounds.* | *Pound.* | *Calories.* |
| Codfish, whole, fresh....... | 10 | 0.90 | 48 | 1.000 | 0.111 | 209 |
| Codfish, steaks............. | 12 | .71 | 36 | .833 | .142 | 274 |
| Bluefish.................... | 12 | 1.20 | 58 | .833 | .083 | 172 |
| Halibut ................... | 18 | 1.18 | 40 | .556 | .085 | 253 |
| Codfish, salt .............. | 7 | .44 | 23 | 1.429 | .229 | 437 |
| Mackerel, salt............. | 10 | ·61 | 10 | 1.000 | .163 | 998 |
| Salmon, canned ........... | 12 | .62 | 18 | .833 | .162 | 547 |
| Oysters (solids, 30 cents quart)..................... | 15 | 2.50 | 68 | .667 | .040 | 147 |
| Oysters (solids, 60 cents quart).................... | 30 | 5.00 | 136 | .333 | .020 | 74 |
| Lobster ................... | 18 | 3.05 | 129 | .556 | .033 | 77 |
| Beef, sirloin steak.......... | 25 | 1.52 | 26 | .400 | .066 | 380 |
| Beef, sirloin steak..... .... | 20 | 1.21 | 21 | .500 | .083 | 475 |
| Beef, round............... | 14 | .74 | 16 | .714 | .136 | 615 |
| Beef, stew meat............ | 5 | .38 | 5 | 2.000 | .266 | 1,862 |
| Beef, dried, chipped........ | 25 | .95 | 33 | .400 | .106 | 303 |
| Mutton chops, loin ......... | 20 | 1.48 | 14 | .500 | .068 | 694 |
| Mutton, leg ............... | 22 | 1.46 | 25 | .454 | .069 | 394 |
| Pork, roast, loin........... | 12 | .90 | 10 | .833 | .112 | 1,016 |
| Pork, smoked ham ......... | 22 | 1.55 | 14 | .454 | .064 | 729 |
| Milk (7 cents quart)........ | 3½ | 1.06 | 11 | 2.857 | .094 | 891 |
| Milk (6 cents quart)........ | 3 | .91 | 10 | 3.333 | .110 | 1,040 |
| Wheat flour................ | 3 | .26 | 2 | 3.333 | .380 | 5,363 |
| Corn meal.................. | 2 | .22 | 1 | 5.000 | .460 | 8,055 |
| Potatoes (90 cents bushel). | 1½ | .83 | 5 | 6.667 | .120 | 2,020 |
| Potatoes (45 cents bushel).. | ¾ | .42 | 2 | 13.333 | .240 | 4,040 |
| Cabbage. ................. | 2½ | 1.79 | 21 | 4.000 | .056 | 484 |
| Corn, canned............. . | 10 | 3.57 | 23 | 1.000 | .028 | 444 |
| Apples.................... | 1½ | 5.00 | 7 | 6.667 | .020 | 1,420 |
| Bananas ................... | 7 | 8.75 | 27 | 1.429 | .011 | 414 |
| Strawberries .............. | 7 | 7.78 | 42 | 1.429 | .013 | 240 |

In the table the prices per pound have been selected from the best data available. It is of course impossible to set any one price which shall represent the cost of these materials per pound in all sections of the country and at all times of the year. It is probable that the prices given represent more nearly those found in the eastern part of the United States than in the southern, central, and western sections, where some food materials are usually somewhat cheaper.

It is to be noted that the cost of 1 pound of protein and 1,000 calories of energy have no direct relation to each other. A pound of protein would be sufficient for a workingman about four days, while 1,000 calories of energy would be less than one-third the amount required per day. By dividing the cost of 1 pound of protein by 4 and multiplying the cost of 1,000 calories of energy by 3.5, results are obtained which show approximately the relative cost of the protein and energy sufficient for one day as furnished by the different food materials. Thus it would take, in round numbers, 25 cents' worth of salt mackerel at 10 cents a pound to furnish one day's supply of protein, while the corresponding energy would require 38 cents' worth. Seven cents' worth of flour would furnish the protein and 5 cents' worth the energy required for one day. It is of course understood that no one food material could furnish the nutrients in their proper proportions for adults under ordinary conditions of health and activity. The values expressed in the table simply show the relative value from a pecuniary standpoint of the different foods as a source of protein on the one hand and of energy on the other.

It will be seen from the above table that at 25 cents a pound it would take $1.52 worth of sirloin steak to furnish a pound of protein, while the same amount could be obtained in 74 cents' worth of beef round at 14 cents a pound, 71 cents' worth of cod steak at 12 cents a pound, 44 cents' worth of salt cod at 7 cents a pound, or 26 cents' worth of wheat flour at 3 cents a pound. In like manner the cost of 1,000 calories of energy would vary in these same food materials from 36 cents, as furnished by the cod steaks, to 2 cents as furnished by the flour.

It is evident that at the prices given the fruits are the most expensive sources of protein, mollusks and crustaceans next, and the cheaper meats and fish, with the cereals, the least expensive. As regards energy, on the other hand, mollusks and crustaceans are by far the most expensive sources, followed by fish and many kinds of meat, while the cereals are the most economical.

## DIGESTIBILITY OF FISH.

The term digestibility, as commonly employed, has several significations. To many persons it conveys the idea that a particular food agrees with the user. It is also very commonly understood to refer to ease or rapidity of digestion. One food is often said to be preferable to another because it is more digestible — *i.e.*, is digested in less time in the stomach, or is apparently digested more readily. A third meaning, and one which is usually understood in scientific treatises on such subjects, refers to the completeness of digestion. For instance, two foods may have the same composition, but, owing to differences in mechanical condition or some other factor, one may be much more completely digestible than the other — that is, give up more material to the body in its passage through the intestinal tract.

The agreement or disagreement of a particular food with any person in normal health is largely a matter of individual peculiarity. When foods habitually disagree with a person, and there is reason to believe that there is pronounced indigestion the advice of a competent physician is needed, since the nourishment of an abnormal or diseased body is a matter properly included under the practice of medicine.

In so far as ease or rapidity of digestion implies a saving of energy to the body, it may be a matter of importance, especially if the energy expenditure would otherwise be above the normal. However, little is known concerning relative rapidity of digestion within the body. Most of the current statements which refer to this are apparently based on experiments carried on outside the body by methods of artificial digestion. Such experiments imitate as closely as possible the conditions in the body, but it is not at all certain that they are exactly the same. Some experiments with man, which were made a good many years ago, before experimental methods had become fixed, are also often quoted, but it is only fair to say that the popular interpretation of the data recorded does not agree in many respects with that of trained investigators.

The numerous artificial digestion experiments which have been made with fish indicate that it is less quickly digested than beef, being about equal to lamb in this respect. However, as compared with other foods, the difference in the digestibility of fish and meat, as shown by these experiments, is not very great. In some carefully conducted experiments, which were reported only a few years ago by a German investigator, it was noted that oysters, whitefish, and shellfish, taken in moderate amounts, left the stomach in two to three hours, in this respect resembling eggs, milk, white bread, and some other foods. Caviar left the stomach in three to four hours, as did also chicken, lean beef, boiled ham, beefsteak, coarse bread, etc. Salt herring left the stomach in four to five hours, other foods in the same class being smoked tongue, roast beef, roast goose, lentil porridge, and peas porridge. So far as fish is concerned, the general deduction from these experiments was that it is more rapidly digested than meat. With respect to its rapidity of digestion in the stomach, another German investigator includes whitefish in the same class as the following animal foods: Roast chicken, pigeon, roast veal, and cold underdone roast beef.

Before sweeping deductions are made the thoroughness with which fish is digested should also be taken into account. A number of experiments have been made with man to learn how thoroughly fish is digested and to compare it in this respect with other foods. In these experiments the food and the feces were analyzed. Deducting the nutritive material excreted in the feces from the total amount consumed in the food showed how much was retained by the body. It was found that fish and lean beef were about equally digestible. In each case about 95 per cent of the total dry matter, 97 per cent of the protein, and over 90 per cent of the fat were retained by the body. Other experiments of the same character indicate that salt fish is less thoroughly digested than fresh fish.

At the Connecticut (Storrs) Station Milner studied the digestibility of fresh (canned) salmon, a typical fat fish, and fresh cod, a typical lean fish, these materials each constituting a considerable part of a simple mixed diet. The calculated coefficients of digestibility of the salmon alone were protein 96.2 per cent and fat 97 per cent, while 85.6 per cent of the energy was available. In the case of the cod the values for protein and fat were 95.9 and 97.4 per cent, respectively, and for energy 80.3 per cent. It has been suggested that fat fish is less thoroughly digested than lean fish, but in these experiments the two sorts were digested on an average with practically the same thoroughness.

A number of similar experiments have been made on the

digestibility of milk, eggs, bread, potatoes, and other animal and vegetable foods. From a large amount of data of this sort some general deductions have been drawn. Thus, it has been calculated that 97 per cent of the protein and 95 per cent of the fat of meats, fish, eggs, dairy products, and the animal food of a mixed diet are digested. Similar values are for the protein of cereals 85 per cent, for the fat 90 per cent, and for the carbohydrates 98 per cent; and for the protein, fat, and carbohydrates of vegetables 83, 90, and 95 per cent, respectively, and for the protein, fat, and carbohydrates of the total vegetable food of a mixed diet 84, 90, and 97 per cent. From the available experimental data it also seems probable that leaner meats are more easily digested than those containing more fat, and the leaner kinds of fish, such as cod, haddock, perch, pike, bluefish, etc., are more easily and readily digested than the fatter kinds, as salmon, shad, and mackerel. Generally speaking, it has been found that the protein of vegetable foods as served on the table is less digestible than that of animal foods. For instance, one-fourth or more of the protein of potatoes and beans may escape digestion and thus be useless for nourishment. This is perhaps entirely due to the mechanical condition in which the protein occurs in vegetable foods; that is, it is often inclosed in cells which have hard walls and are not acted upon by the digestive juices. It is ordinarily assumed that the small amount of carbohydrates in meat and fish is entirely digested. Carbohydrates other than fiber, which make up the larger part of the vegetable foods, are very digestible. The fat in both animal and vegetable foods differs in digestibility under varying conditions. No marked difference in the digestibility of the fat in the two classes of food can be pointed out.

Persons differ in respect to the action of foods in the digestive apparatus; and fish, like other food materials, is subject to these influences of personal peculiarity.

The nutritive value of shellfish, as of other fish, depends to a considerable extent upon its digestibility, but information on this point is so limited that but little can be said with certainty here. Perhaps the most that can be said is that while there are people with whom such foods do not always agree, yet oysters belong to the more easily digestible class of foods. In a recently published study of the composition of the oyster and other problems connected with their food value, the statement is made that the nutrients occur largely in forms in which they are readily assimilated, as is shown by the fact that one-half of the crushed oyster and one-fourth of the whole oyster is soluble in water.  So far as can be learned no experiments have been made which show how thoroughly clams, crabs, and other crustacea, turtle, and terrapin, and frogs' legs are digested.

## PLACE OF FISH IN THE DIET.

The chief uses of fish as food are (1) to furnish an economical source of nitrogenous nutrients and (2) to supply the demand for variety in the diet, which increases with the advance of civilization.

Inspection of a considerable number of dietary studies of families of farmers, mechanics, professional men, and others, carried on in different regions of the United States, shows that about 20 per cent of the total food, 43 per cent of the total protein, and 55 per cent of the total fat of the diet of the average family is obtained from meats, poultry, fish, shellfish, etc., together.  Fish, shellfish, etc., alone furnish less than 3 per cent of the total food, less than 4 per cent of the total protein, and less than 1 per cent of the total fat, showing to what a limited extent such food is used in the average household.  It is not improbable that in communities where fisheries constitute the principal industry much larger quantities are · consumed.  It has been found that the laborers employed in the fisheries in Russia consume from 26 to 62 ounces of fish daily.  This, with some bread, millet meal, and tea, constitutes the diet throughout the fishing season.  These quantities are unusually large, but no bad effects are mentioned as following the diet.

There is a widespread notion that fish contains large proportions of phosphorus, and on that account is particularly valuable as brain food.  The percentages of phosphorus in specimens thus far analyzed are not larger than are found in the flesh of other animals used for food.  But, even if the flesh be richer in phosphorus, there is no experimental evidence to warrant the assumption that fish is more valuable than meats or other food material for the nourishment of the brain.

The opinion of eminent physiologists is that phosphorus is no more essential to the brain than nitrogen, potassium, or any other element which occurs in its tissues.  The value commonly attributed to the phosphorus is based on a popular misconception of statements by one of the early writers on such topics. In discussing the belief that " fish contains certain elements which are adapted in a special manner to renovate the brain and so to support mental labor " a prominent physiologist says, " There is no foundation whatever for this view."

It is well understood that persons in varying conditions of life and occupation require different kinds and quantities of food. For the laboring man doing heavy work the diet must contain a comparatively large amount of the fuel ingredients and enough of the flesh-forming substances to make good the wear and tear of the body. These materials are all present in the flesh of animals, but not in the requisite proportions. Fish and the leaner kinds of meat are deficient in materials which yield heat and muscular power. When, however, fish and meat are supplemented by bread, potatoes, etc., a diet is provided which will supply all the demands of the body. Where fish can be obtained at low cost it may advantageously furnish a considerable portion of the protein required, and under most conditions its use may be profitably extended solely on the plea of variety.

It should be stated that most physiologists regard fish as a particularly desirable food for persons of sedentary habits, because it seems to be less " hearty." While, so far as can be learned, such statements do not depend upon experimental evidence, they are thought to embody the result of experience.

## PREPARING FISH FOR THE TABLE.

Fish is prepared for the table in a variety of ways, which are described in detail in books devoted to cookery. A few words, however, may not be inappropriate on the general methods of cooking and possible loss of nutrients involved.

Fish is commonly boiled, steamed, broiled, fried, or baked, or may be combined with other materials in some made dish. When boiled, it is stated that the loss in weight ranges from 5 to 30 per cent. One experimenter gives 26 per cent as the average. This loss is largely made up of water — that is, the cooked fish is much less moist than the raw. Little fat or protein is lost. So far as known, experiments have not been made which show the losses by other methods of cooking. It is, however, probable that there would be usually a very considerable loss of water.

In most cases fat or carbohydrates in the form of butter, flour, or other material are added to fish when cooked, and thus the deficiency in fuel ingredients is made good. Boiled or steamed fish is often accompanied by a rich sauce, made from butter, eggs, etc. Fried fish is cooked in fat, and baked fish is often filled with force meat, and may also be accompanied by a sauce ; the force meat being made of bread, butter, etc., contains fat and carbohydrates. In made dishes — chowders, fish, pies, salads, etc. — fat and carbohydrates (butter, flour, vegetables, etc.) are combined with fish, the kind and amount varying in the individual cases. Furthermore, in the ordinary household, fish or meat is supplemented by such foods as bread, butter, potatoes, green vegetables, and fruit. That is, by adding materials in cooking and by serving other dishes with the cooked product the protein of the fish is supplemented by the necessary fat and carbohydrates.

## DAILY MENUS CONTAINING FISH.

By taking into account the chemical composition of a mixed diet and comparing it with accepted dietary standards it may be seen whether the diet is actually suited to the requirements of the body ; that is, whether it supplies sufficient protein and energy and whether it supplies them in the right proportions.

A number of sample menus are given on pages 32 to 36, which show that the desired amounts of protein and energy may be readily supplied by a diet containing a considerable amount of fish. These menus (which are based in part on dietary studies and other food investigations of this Department covering a wide range and extending over several years) are not intended as formulas for any family to follow, but simply as illustrations of the way in which menus containing the proper proportions of nutrients may be made up. The ingenuity of the housewife and her knowledge of the tastes of the family will suggest the special dishes and combinations suited to her needs. It is not assumed that any housewife will find it convenient to follow exactly the proportions suggested in the menus. The purpose is to show her about what amounts and proportions of food materials would give the required nutrients.

In selecting these menus it has been the object to include

such amounts of fish as might be commonly served in an ordinary household and not to provide meals with the largest possible quantity of fish. That the amount which it is possible to introduce in a single meal may be large is shown by the "shore dinners" so common in some regions of New England, or by the famous dinners served at Greenwich on the Thames, with six courses and fish in every course.

With reference to the following menus several points should be borne in mind. The amounts given represent about what would be called for in a family whose demand for food would be equivalent to four full-grown men at light to moderate manual labor, such as machinists, carpenters, mill workers, farmers, truckmen, etc., according to the usually accepted dietary standards. It is ordinarily assumed that an average man in health performing light to moderate muscular work requires per day about .25 pound protein and 3,050 calories of energy, the latter being supplied in small part by protein, but mostly by fat and carbohydrates. Men in professional life, performing less muscular work, require smaller amounts. The commonly accepted American dietary standard for such men calls for .22 pound protein and 2,700 calories of energy in the daily food. The amount of mineral matter required is not stated, since there is little accurate information available on this point. A diet made up of ordinary foods and supplying the necessary amounts of protein and energy would undoubtedly supply an abundance of mineral matter.

It has been found that women and children consume somewhat less food than men. The assumption is usually made that, provided a woman is engaged in some moderately active occupation, she requires about eight-tenths as much food as a man with a similar amount of work.

In calculating the results of dietary studies (which may be most conveniently expressed in amounts for one man for one day), it is further assumed that a boy 13 to 14 years old and a girl 15 to 16 years old also require about eight-tenths as much food as a man at moderately active muscular labor; a boy of 12 and a girl 13 to 14 years old, about seven-tenths; a boy 10 to 11 and a girl 10 to 12 years old, about six-tenths; a child 6 to 9 years old, about five-tenths; one 2 to 5, about four-tenths, and an infant under 2 years, about three-tenths.

As previously stated, the quantities in the sample menus are for four men at moderately active muscular work or an equivalent number of men, women, and children. A family might, for example, consist of a mechanic and wife, with four children, two girls of 12 and 6 and two boys of 10 and 8 years, respectively. Here it would be assumed that the man would be engaged at moderately hard manual work. According to the above factors, this family would be equal in food consumption to 4 men at moderate muscular exercise (1.0+0.8+0.6+0.6+0.5+0.5=4). In the same way a day laborer's family, consisting of a father and mother with three children under 7 years of age, would be equivalent to 3 men with moderate muscular exercise (1.0+0.8+0.5+0.4+0.3=3), and would require three-fourths the quantities indicated in the following menus:

MENU I. — *For family equivalent to four men at light to moderate muscular work.*

| Food Material. | Amount Used. | | Protein. | Fuel Value. |
|---|---|---|---|---|
| **BREAKFAST.** | *Lbs.* | *oz.* | *Pound.* | *Calories.* |
| Oranges.......................... | 2 | 0 | 0.012 | 338 |
| Omelet (8 eggs) .................. | 1 | 0 | .131 | 613 |
|    Butter for frying................ | 0 | 1 | .001 | 216 |
| Johnnycake * · ................... | 1 | 4 | .099 | 1,466 |
|    Butter ......................... | 0 | 3 | .002 | 647 |
| Coffee ............................ | .......... | | .008 | 248 |
|     Total ..................... | .......... | | .253 | 3,528 |
| **DINNER.** | | | | |
| Boiled cod, fresh.................. | 2 | 0 | .340 | 658 |
| Hollandaise sauce: | | | | |
|    Butter ....................... | 0 | 4 | .002 | 863 |
|    Yolks of 2 eggs ............... | 0 | 1½ | .013 | 135 |
|    Lemon juice, etc. ............. | .......... | | .......... | ........ |
| Potatoes ......................... | 2 | 0 | .036 | 606 |
| Boiled rice † ..................... | 1 | 8 | .018 | 362 |
| Milk ............................. | 0 | 6 | .012 | 117 |
| Sugar............................. | 0 | 3 | ......... | 340 |
| Bread............................. | 0 | 12 | .069 | 887 |
| Butter ........................... | 0 | 3 | .002 | 647 |
|     Total ..................... | .......... | | .492 | 4,615 |

MENU I. — *Continued.*

| Food Material. | Amount Used. | | Protein. | Fuel Value. |
|---|---|---|---|---|
| **SUPPER.** | | | | |
| Scalloped oysters : | *Lbs.* | *oz.* | *Pound.* | *Calories.* |
| Oysters ........................ | 2 | 0 | .120 | 442 |
| Crackers ...................... | 0 | 4 | .027 | 464 |
| Butter ........................ | 0 | 2 | .001 | 431 |
| Milk ......................... | 0 | 4 | .008 | 78 |
| French fried potatoes................ | 1 | 0 | .018 | 303 |
| Lard ......................... | 0 | 2 | ............ | 505 |
| Bread......................... | 0 | 8 | .046 | 592 |
| Butter ....................... | 0 | 2 | ............ | 431 |
| Sliced bananas.................... | 1 | 0 | .008 | 290 |
| Sugar......................... | 0 | 3 | ............ | 340 |
| Tea........................... | ............ | | .008 | 248 |
| Total ....................... | ............ | | .237 | 4,124 |
| Total per day.................. | ............ | | .982 | 12,267 |
| Total for one man.............. | ............ | | .246 | 3,067 |

\* Composition of cooked material from U.S. Dept. Agr., Office of Experiment Stations Bul. 28, revised.

† Composition of cooked material from unpublished data.

MENU II. — *For family equivalent to four men at light to moderate muscular work.*

| Food Material. | Amount Used. | | Protein. | Fuel Value. |
|---|---|---|---|---|
| **BREAKFAST.** | | | | |
| Codfish creamed : | *Lbs.* | *oz.* | *Pounds.* | *Calories.* |
| Salt cod....................... | 0 | 8 | 0.080 | 153 |
| Milk.......................... | 1 | 0 | .033 | 312 |
| Butter ........................ | 0 | 1 | .001 | 216 |
| Flour ......................... | 0 | 1 | .007 | 101 |
| Baked potatoes *.................... | 1 | 12 | .044 | 721 |
| Bread.......................... | 0 | 12 | .069 | 887 |
| Butter ........................ | 0 | 4 | .002 | 863 |
| Coffee ......................... | ............ | | .008 | 248 |
| Total ........................ | ............ | | .244 | 3,501 |

## MENU II. — *Continued.*

| Food Material. | Amount Used. | | Protein. | Fuel Value. |
|---|---|---|---|---|
| | *Lbs.* | *oz.* | *Pounds.* | *Calories.* |
| **DINNER.** | | | | |
| Clam soup : | | | | |
| Clams, round.................... | 0 | 12 | .049 | 158 |
| Milk ......................... | 1 | 12 | .057 | 545 |
| Butter ......................... | 0 | 1½ | .001 | 324 |
| Flour ......................... | 0 | 1 | .007 | 101 |
| Onion, salt, pepper, etc........... | ......... | ......... | ......... | ......... |
| Roast lamb, leg †.............. | 1 | 8 | .238 | 1,256 |
| Green peas ‡.................... | 1 | 8 | .054 | 377 |
| Butter ......................... | 0 | 2 | .001 | 431 |
| Mashed potatoes *.............. | 1 | 8 | .039 | 737 |
| Bread........................ | 0 | 6 | .034 | 444 |
| Butter ......................... | 0 | 1 | .001 | 216 |
| Apple tapioca pudding.............. | 1 | 0 | .003 | 541 |
| Total ...................... | ......... | | .484 | 5,130 |
| **SUPPER.** | | | | |
| Lobster salad : | | | | |
| Lobster meat................. | 1 | 0 | .164 | 377 |
| Yolks of 3 eggs ................ | 0 | 2 | .020 | 202 |
| Butter **or** oil.................... | 0 | 3 | .002 | 647 |
| Milk......................... | 0 | 7 | .014 | 137 |
| Sugar......................... | 0 | 1 | ......... | 113 |
| (Vinegar, salt, pepper, mustard)... | ......... | ......... | ......... | ......... |
| Biscuit........................ | 0 | 12 | .065 | 950 |
| Butter ........................ | 0 | 4 | .003 | 863 |
| Tea ......................... | ......... | | .008 | 248 |
| Total ...................... | ......... | | .276 | 3,537 |
| Total per day................. | ......... | | 1.004 | 12,168 |
| Total for one man............. | ......... | | .251 | 3,042 |

\* Composition of cooked material from U.S. Dept. Agr., Office of Experiment Stations Bul. 28, revised.

† A larger piece would ordinarily be cooked. The amount given is for one meal.

‡ Weight with pods.

MENU III. — *For family equivalent to four men at light to moderate muscular work.*

| Food Material. | Amount Used. | | Protein. | Fuel Value. |
|---|---|---|---|---|
| | *Lbs.* | *oz.* | *Pounds.* | *Calories.* |
| **BREAKFAST.** | | | | |
| Breakfast cereal : | | | | |
| Cracked crushed wheat.......... | 0 | 4 | 0.028 | 410 |
| Milk...................... | 0 | 6 | .012 | 117 |
| Sugar..................... | 0 | 2 | ......... | 227 |
| Creamed dried beef : | | | | |
| Dried beef .................. | 0 | 12 | .198 | 568 |
| Milk...................... | 0 | 8 | .017 | 156 |
| Butter .................... | 0 | 1 | .001 | 216 |
| French fried potatoes ............ | 1 | 0 | .018 | 303 |
| Butter (taken up in frying)...... | 0 | 2 | .001 | 431 |
| Bread .................... | 0 | 12 | .069 | 887 |
| Butter ................... | 0 | 3 | .002 | 647 |
| Coffee ................... | ......... | | .008 | 248 |
| Total ................ | ......... | | .354 | 4,210 |
| **DINNER.** | | | | |
| Halibut steak............... | 1 | 12 | 0.268 | 796 |
| Mashed potatoes *............ | 2 | 0 | .052 | 982 |
| Tomatoes (or half amount of parsnips) | 2 | 0 | .018 | 206 |
| Bread .................... | 0 | 12 | .069 | 887 |
| Butter ................... | 0 | 3 | .003 | 647 |
| Apple pie ................. | 1 | 0 | .031 | 1,228 |
| Total ................ | ......... | | .441 | 4.746 |
| **SUPPER.** | | | | |
| Salmon croquettes : | | | | |
| Canned salmon *............ | 0 | 8 | .098 | 328 |
| Mashed potatoes †............ | 1 | 0 | .026 | 491 |
| Butter ................... | 0 | 1 | .001 | 216 |
| 1 egg ................... | 0 | 2 | .016 | 77 |
| Prune sauce †............... | 1 | 0 | .005 | 418 |
| Muffins................... | 0 | 12 | .065 | 950 |
| Butter ................... | 0 | 3 | .002 | 647 |
| Tea...................... | ......... | | .008 | 248 |
| Total ................ | ......... | | .221 | 3,375 |
| Total per day............... | ......... | | 1.016 | 12,331 |
| Total for one man............ | ......... | | .254 | 3,083 |

*Composition of cooked material from U.S. Dept. Agr., Office of Experiment Stations Bul. 28, revised.

† Composition of cooked material from unpublished data.

Menu IV. — *For family equivalent to four men at light to moderate muscular work.*

| Food Material. | Amount Used. | | Protein. | Fuel Value. |
|---|---|---|---|---|
| **BREAKFAST.** | Lbs. | oz. | Pound. | Calories. |
| Breakfast cereal : | | | | |
|   Cracked crushed wheat.......... | 0 | 4 | 0.028 | 410 |
|   Milk..................... | 0 | 6 | .012 | 117 |
|   Sugar................... | 0 | 2 | ......... | 227 |
| Broiled salt mackerel............... | 1 | 6 | .191 | 1,524 |
| Boiled potatoes ................... | 1 | 0 | .018 | 303 |
| Hot rolls ....................... | 0 | 12 | .067 | 1,017 |
| Butter ......................... | 0 | 3 | .002 | 647 |
| Coffee ......................... | ......... | | .008 | 248 |
|    Total ..................... | ......... | | .326 | 4,493 |
| **DINNER.** | | | | |
| Broiled beefsteak.................. | 1 | 8 | .248 | 1,424 |
| Baked potatoes *.................. | 1 | 8 | .038 | 618 |
| Onions......................... | 2 | 0 | .028 | 398 |
| Celery ......................... | 1 | 0 | .009 | 68 |
| Bread........................... | 0 | 12 | .069 | 887 |
| Butter ......................... | 0 | 3 | .002 | 647 |
| Baked apples : | | | | |
|   Apples....................... | 1 | 0 | .003 | 213 |
|   Sugar....................... | 0 | 2 | ......... | 227 |
|   Milk ....................... | 0 | 4 | .008 | 78 |
|    Total ..................... | ......... | | .405 | 4,560 |
| **SUPPER.** | | | | |
| Oyster stew : | | | | |
|   1¼ pints oysters ................. | 1 | 4 | .075 | 276 |
|   1 pint milk ..................... | 1 | 0 | .033 | 312 |
|   Butter ....................... | 0 | 1 | .001 | 215 |
| Crackers....................... | 0 | 6 | .042 | 716 |
| Bread........................... | 0 | 8 | .046 | 592 |
| Butter ......................... | 0 | 2 | .001 | 431 |
| Chocolate layer cake ................ | 0 | 8 | .031 | 801 |
| Tea............................ | ......... | | .008 | 248 |
|    Total ..................... | ......... | | .237 | 3,591 |
|    Total per day................. | ......... | | .968 | 12,644 |
|    Total for one man ............ | ......... | | .242 | 3,161 |

* Percentage composition of cooked material from unpublished data.

The weights of fish, meats, and vegetables given in the menus are for these articles as found in the market. The fish and meats will include, as a rule, more or less bone, and the vegetables considerable skin and other parts which are inedible and are rejected. In estimating the nutrients allowance is made for what has been found to be the average proportion of bone in different cuts of meats. In vegetables it is assumed that from one-sixth to one-fifth will be rejected in preparing them for the table. The weights of the breakfast cereals are for these in the dry condition before cooking.

The values given for tea or coffee are obtained by taking account of the sugar and milk or cream consumed with them. The infusion of tea or coffee contains little, if any, nutritive material. The value of tea and coffee in the diet depends upon their agreeable flavor and mild stimulating properties.

The calculations of the quantities of nutrients contained in the different foods are based upon the average percentage composition of these materials, some of the data being included in the table of composition on page 10, and the remainder in a previous publication of this Office.*

The fats and carbohydrates in the different food materials are not shown in the menus, since the quantity of protein and the fuel value of the food are the values which are of special interest. The fuel value of the fats and carbohydrates is, of course, included in the figures for fuel value given.

In the menus only such an amount of each food is indicated as might be completely consumed at each meal. Of course, in the ordinary household usually a rather larger quantity of the different dishes will be prepared than will be consumed at one meal, but the thrifty housekeeper will see to it that what is not used at one meal will be utilized for another.

It is not expected that each meal or the total food of each individual day will have just the amounts of protein and fuel ingredients that make a well-balanced diet. The body is continually storing nutritive materials and using them. It is a repository of nutriment which is being constantly drawn upon and as constantly resupplied. It is not dependent any day upon the food eaten that particular day. Hence an excess one day may be made up by a deficiency the next or vice versa. Healthful nourishment requires simply that the

*U.S. Dept. Agr., Office of Experiment Stations Bul. 28, revised.

nutrients as a whole during longer or shorter periods should be fitted to the actual needs of the body.

It will be seen that in each of the menus suggested fish occurs in at least two meals. However, in no case is the amount greater than experience has shown may commonly occur in actual dietaries. It is not the intention to suggest that a diet containing such quantities of fish be followed every day, but rather to show that fish may be readily combined with other food materials to supply the protein and energy required. While it may profitably be used more frequently in many families than is at present the case, the quantity used is a matter to be settled by the demands of individual taste.

The menus attempt to cover, as regards fish and other materials, a range in variety and combination such as might be found in an average well-to-do household. Other dishes, such as fish soups, chowders, fish salads, etc., might have been included also, and would naturally find a place on the table of a family fond of fish and fish products. Individual preferences vary so much that no combination which could be selected would meet them all.

Nothing has been said of the cost of the food used in the menus. All foods vary in price in different localities, and this is especially the case with fish. In general it may be said that a large variety of fruits, green vegetables, etc., if it is necessary to purchase them, increases the cost of a diet out of proportion to the nutritive material furnished. Such foods, however, are valuable, since they possess agreeable flavor and so render the diet appetizing. It is also generally believed that the acids, salts, and similar materials in fruits and vegetables are of value in maintaining the body in health. The income of the purchaser should determine how varied the diet may be.

Fish may contain parasites, some of which are injurious to man. These are, however, destroyed by the thorough cooking to which fish is usually subjected.

Ptomaines are poisonous bodies due to the action of microörganisms. They are chemical compounds of definite compounds and are elaborated by microörganisms breaking down the complex ingredients of animal tissues, just as alcohol is due to the action of yeasts breaking down sugar, or as acetic acid is formed from the alcohol of cider or wine by the yeast-like plant which produces vinegar, and which we call mother when we find it collected in masses. The formation of ptomaines quite generally, although not always, accompanies putrefaction (being greatest, it is said, in its early stages), and therefore great care should be taken to eat fish only when it is in perfectly good condition. Fish which has been frozen and, after thawing, kept for a time before it is cooked, is especially likely to contain injurious ptomaines.

Decomposition can often be recognized by the odor of the fish, especially when it has progressed to any considerable extent. There are laboratory tests for showing decomposition at various stages and for indicating the presence of ptomaines.

Salt water fish are in supply the entire year, that is, there are no closed seasons. To be good they must be solid with meat firm. The fresher they are the firmer will be the meat. Frozen fish should not be thawed out till ready to use and then a soaking for 1 to 2 hours in cold water is generally sufficient to remove the frost.

If gills are in the fish they should be red. Bleached out gills are stale and the fish containing them may also be so considered.

Eyes are another source to tell good fish. The fish when new contain bright clear eyes and the duller the eye the older the fish.

The first place a fish will spoil will be along the back bone where blood lays. If that does not smell and looks fresh you can be sure the goods are fresh and fit to eat.

### REMARKS IN REGARD TO FISH.

Fish should never stand in water, as it spoils the flavor. Fish should never be fried in butter. It should always be used while fresh. Plain boiled or mashed potatoes should always be served with it. Squash and green peas go very well with fish also. Always save all that remains after a meal, and warm up, to help out another dish. The remains of boiled fresh fish can be warmed up in a little butter, pepper, salt, and water, as you would stew lobster. Cold fried and broiled fish can be placed in a tin pan, and set into the oven ten minutes, when it will be found to be hot enough. Fish balls can be steamed for ten or fifteen minutes, and then set into the oven to get crisp. If you have a large piece of boiled fish, which you wish to serve whole, place it on a plate, and set into the steamer, and steam twenty minutes. If you have drawn butter to warm up, do not set it on the fire, but put into a bowl, and set the bowl into hot water. Cook butter as little as possible, as by cooking it becomes oily. When you do use it, always add it three or five minutes before taking the dish from the fire.

Laying fish in water has been recommended as a means of judging of their condition. Those which sink may be considered undecomposed and wholesome, while those which are decomposing will float.

Canned fish should never be allowed to remain long in the can after opening, but should be used at once. There is some possibility of danger from the combined action of the can contents and oxygen of the air upon the lead of the solder or the can itself. Furthermore, canned fish seems peculiarly suited to the growth of microörganisms when exposed to the air.

Finally, fish offered for sale should be handled in a cleanly manner, and stored and exposed for sale under hygienic conditions.

A kind of poisoning called mytilism, usually very fatal in its results, has been sometimes observed to follow the eating of clams. The reason for this illness is not definitely known, though it is attributed to a poisonous body sometimes found in clams, especially in the liver. Just why this poisonous body occurs is not known, but it is probably due to a disease or some abnormal condition; furthermore, it has been noted that clams from some regions are quite uniformly poisonous. It is said that poisonous clams are less pigmented (lighter with radiate streaks) than wholesome clams, which are uniformly darkly pigmented, and that the shells of the unwholesome clams are more friable and broader, and that the liver is larger, softer, and richer in pigment and fat. A well-known writer on the subject recommends that the public should be warned against buying dead clams — that is, those which do not close the shell when taken out of the water — and that as a further precaution the liver and the broth should not be eaten, if cases of mytilism have recently occurred locally or there is any other reason to suspect the clam supply.

Slight or serious poisoning has also been known to follow the eating of oysters, though fortunately American oysters have been seldom found to be a cause of such illness. As in the case of clams, the reason for such illness is not definitely known, but it is probably due to the occasional presence in oysters of some poisonous body due to disease or a similar cause. An European investigator reached the conclusion that oysters are generally diseased in the summer months, though the nature of the disease was not learned. He found that the diseased oysters possessed a characteristic milky appearance and that the liver was much enlarged, gray, and soft. It does not seem probable that American oysters are generally diseased during the summer months, as many who live in the oyster-producing regions eat them throughout the year, yet in view of the fact that bad results from eating shellfish are more frequently noticed in the summer than in the cooler months, possibly because they spoil more readily, omitting them from the bill of fare during the summer seems a wise precaution. Oysters dead in the shell or those which are decomposed should under no circumstances be eaten. When removed from the water good oysters close the shell, move when touched, are of normal size and color, and have a clear fluid inside the shell. In the case of oysters dead when taken from the water, the shells remain open, while those which are decomposed are discolored and very soft, have a stale odor, and show a blackish ring on the inside of the shell.

Oyster beds should be free from sewage pollution, and oysters when " floated " or " fattened " should never be placed in water contaminated by sewage. Severe illness and death have resulted in many cases from eating raw oysters contaminated with sewage containing typhoid fever germs.

It is only just to say that the dangers from parasites, microorganisms, ptomaines, and uncleanly surroundings are not limited to fish. Under conditions which favor the growth of the microörganisms, meat and other highly nitrogenous animal foods undergo decomposition resulting in the formation of ptomaines. Animal parasites may be acquired from flesh of various kinds if not thoroughly cooked, provided, of course, the flesh is infested. This danger is reduced by proper inspection. Vegetable foods also may become contaminated in various ways. The importance of measures to secure pure and wholesome food can hardly be overstated. The best interests of the people undoubtedly demand a strict and impartial supervision by public officers of the sale of food products.

# Advice to the Cook.

Great cleanliness, as well as care and attention, is required from a cook. Keep your hands *very* clean; try to prevent your nails from getting black or discolored; don't "scatter" in your kitchen; clean up as you go; put cold water into each saucepan or stewpan as you finish using it. Dry your saucepans before you put them on the shelf. Scour tins with good mineral soap and rinse thoroughly in hot water. In cleaning a frying-pan, scour the *outside* as well as the inside. In cleaning greasy utensils, such as the soup-pot and frying-pan, wipe off the worst of the grease with soft paper (which can be burned), then soak in warm water to which soap-powder or a little ammonia has been added, finishing with mineral soap. Wash your pudding-cloths, *scald* and hang them to dry directly after using them; air them before you put them away, or they will be musty; keep in dry place. Be careful not to use a knife that has cut onions till it has been cleaned. Keep sink and sink-brush very clean; be careful never to throw anything but water down sink. Do not throw cabbage water down it; throw it away out of doors; its smell is very bad. Never have sticky plates or dishes; use very hot water for washing them; when greasy, change it. Take care that you look at the meat the butcher brings, to see that it is good. Let there be no waste in the kitchen.

# Rules for Kitchen.

Without cleanliness and punctuality good cooking is impossible. Leave nothing dirty—clean and clear as you go. A time for everything and everything in time. A good cook wastes nothing. An hour lost in the morning has to be run after all day. Strong fire for roasting. Clear fire for broiling. Wash vegetables in three waters. Boil fish quickly; meat slowly. Throw flour on kerosene flames. Slamming door of oven makes cake fall. A few drops of lemon juice makes cake frosting very white. Try sprinkling powdered cloves about places infected with red ants. Salt in the oven under baking tins will prevent scorching on the bottom. Salt and vinegar will remove stains from discolored teacups.

# Time Tables for the Cook.*

## BOILING

| MEATS | TIME | VEGETABLES | TIME |
|---|---|---|---|
| Chicken, per lb. | 15 min. | Asparagus | 20-30 min. |
| Fowl, per lb. | 20-30 min. | Beets | 30-90 min. |
| Corned Beef, per lb. | 30 min. | Brussels Sprouts | 10-15 min. |
| Ham, per lb. | 18-20 min. | Cabbage | 20 min. |
| Mutton, per lb. | 15 min. | Cauliflower | 20 min. |
| Pot Roast Beef, per lb. | 30-35 min. | Green Corn | 10-20 min. |
| Turkey, per lb. | 15 min. | Lima Beans | 30-40 min. |
| | | Onions | 30-40 min. |
| **FISH** | **TIME** | Parsnips | 30-40 min. |
| Bass, per lb. | 10 min. | Peas | 15-20 min. |
| Blue, per lb. | 10 min. | Potatoes | 20-30 min. |
| Cod, per lb. | 6 min. | Spinach | 15-20 min. |
| Haddock, per lb. | 6 min. | String Beans | 20-30 min. |
| Halibut, per lb. | 15 min. | Turnips | 30-60 min. |
| Lobster, per lb. | 30-40 min. | | |
| Salmon, per lb. | 10-15 min. | Macaroni | 20 min. |
| Small Fish, per lb. | 6 min. | Rice | 15-20 min. |

## BAKING.†

| MEATS | TIME | MEATS | TIME |
|---|---|---|---|
| Beef, ribs, rare, per lb. | 10 min. | Birds, small, hot oven | 20 min. |
| Beef, ribs, well done, per lb. | 12 min. | Braised Meats | 3-4 hrs. |
| Beef, ribs, rolled, per lb. | 12 min. | Ducks, Tame | 45 min. |
| Beef, round, per lb. | 12-15 min. | Ducks, Wild, hot oven | 15 min. |
| Chicken, per lb. | 15 min. | Fillet, hot oven | 30 min. |
| Goose, per lb. | 18 min. | Grouse | 20-25 min. |
| Lamb, well done, per lb. | 15 min. | Partridge | 35-40 min. |
| Mutton, leg, rare, per lb. | 10 min. | Turkey, 8 lb. | 1¾ hrs. |
| Mutton, leg, well done, per lb. | 15 min. | Turkey, very large | 3 hrs. |
| Mutton, loin, rare, per lb. | 8 min. | | |
| Mutton, sh'lder stuffed, per lb. | 15 min. | | |
| Mutton, saddle, rare, per lb. | 10 min. | **FISH** | **TIME** |
| Pork, well done, per lb. | 20 min. | Large Fish | 1 hour |
| Veal, well done, per lb. | 18-20 min. | Small Fish | 20-30 min. |
| Venison, rare, per lb. | 10 min. | | |

†Add quarter of an hour to your baking time to give the roast time to heat through.

## BROILING.

| | TIME | | TIME |
|---|---|---|---|
| Steak, 1 inch thick | 8-10 min. | Grouse | 15 min. |
| Steak, 1½ inches thick | 15 min. | Quail | 8-10 min. |
| Mutton Chops, French | 8 min. | Fish, large | 15-25 min. |
| Mutton Chops, English | 10 min. | Fish, small | 5-10 min. |
| Spring Chicken | 20 min. | Squabs | 10-15 min. |

*So much depends upon the age of vegetables and the length of time since gathering, and upon the tenderness or otherwise of meat, that it is hard to give exact figures for their cooking-times. Just here a little experience is worth a book of rules.

# How to Measure.

One cup, or one tablespoon, or one teaspoon, means a full measure—all it will hold of liquid, and even with the rim, or edge, of dry material.

Stir up all packed materials, like mustard, in its box, and sift flour before measuring. Fill cup without shaking down, and dip spoon in material, taking up a heaped measure, then with a knife scrap off toward the tip till you have level measure. Pack butter or cottolene in cup so there will be no air spaces. A **scant cup** means one-eighth less and a **heaped cup** about one-eighth more than a level cup.

Divide a level spoon lengthwise for a **half measure,** and a half spoon crosswise for quarters or eighths. A **pinch** means about one-eighth, so does a saltspoon; less than that means a **dash** or a few grains.

A **rounded tablespoon** means filled above the rim as much as the spoon hollow below, and equals two of level measure. It also equals one ounce in weight, and two rounded tablespoons if put together would heap a tablespoon about as high as would an egg, giving us the old-time measure of "butter size of an egg," or two ounces, or one-fourth the cup. Butter and flour for sauces are commonly measured by the rounded tablespoon by the experienced housekeeper.

Soda, cream of tartar, baking powder, salt and spices, and some extracts are generally measured with a teaspoon, level measure, for this gives the proportional amount needed for the cup measure of other materials.

# Weights and Measures.

| | |
|---|---|
| 4 gills . . . . . . . . . . . . | 1 pint |
| 2 pints . . . . . . . . . . . | 1 quart |
| 4 quarts . . . . . . . . . . | 1 gallon |
| 16 ounces . . . . . . . . . . | 1 pound |
| ½ kitchen cupful . . . . . . . | 1 gill |
| 1 kitchen cupful . . . . . . . . | ½ pint or 2 gills |
| 4 kitchen cupfuls . . . . . . . | 1 quart |
| 2 cupfuls of granulated sugar . . . . | 1 pound |
| 2½ cupfuls of powdered sugar . . . . | 1 pound |
| 1 heaping tablespoonful of sugar . . . | 1 ounce |

| | |
|---|---|
| 1 heaping tablespoonful of butter . . . . | 2 ounces or ¼ cup |
| Butter size of an egg . . . . . . . . | 2 ounces or ¼ cup |
| 1 cupful of butter . . . . . . . . | ½ pound |
| 4 cupfuls of flour . . . . . . . . | 1 pound |
| 1 heaping quart . . . . . . . . . | 1 pound |
| 8 round tablespoonfuls of dry material . | 1 cupful |
| 16 tablespoonfuls of liquid . . . . . | 1 cupful |

# Table of Measures.

Sixty drops—one teaspoonful.

Three teaspoonfuls—one tablespoonful.

Four tablespoonfuls—one quarter of a cup.

One round tablespoonful butter—one ounce.

One cup solid butter, granulated sugar, or milk—one-half pound.

One scant cup rice—one-half pound.

Two cups flour—one-half pound.

Two heaping cups coffee—one-half pound.

Nine large eggs—one pound.

A cupful means one-half pint.

The old-fashioned china cup is best to use when a half-pint measure is not at hand.

# Proportions.

5 to 8 eggs to 1 quart of milk for custards.

3 to 4 eggs to 1 pint of milk for custards.

1 saltspoonful of salt to one quart of milk for custards.

1 teaspoonful of vanilla to one quart of milk for custards.

2 ounces of gelatine to 1¾ quarts of liquid.

4 heaping tablespoonfuls of corn-starch to one quart of milk.

3 heaping teaspoonfuls of baking powder to one cupful of flour.

1 teaspoonful of soda to one pint of sour milk.

1 teaspoonful of soda to ½ pint of molasses.

1 teaspoonful of baking powder is the equivalent of ½ teaspoonful of soda and 1 teaspoonful of cream of tartar.

# Table of Proportions.

One cup liquid to three cups flour for bread.
One cup liquid to two cups flour for muffins.
One cup liquid to one cup flour for batter.
Liquids scant, flour full measure.
One teaspoonful soda to one pint sour milk.
One teaspoonful soda to one cup molasses.
One-fourth teaspoonful salt to one quart custard.
One teaspoonful salt to one quart water.
One-fourth teaspoonful salt to one cup white sauce.
One-eighth teaspoonful white pepper to one cup white sauce.
One-eighth teaspoonful salt equals one pinch.

# Advice for the Care of Kitchen Utensils.

Attention to details is very necessary.

Sand or bath brick is excellent for cleaning wooden articles, floors, tables, etc.

If you use limestone water an oyster shell in the tea kettle will receive the lime deposit.

Boil in the coffee pot occasionally soap, water, and washing soda. It should always be bright to assure good coffee.

Pans made of sheet iron are better to bake bread in than those made of tin.

If skillets are very greasy a little sal soda in the water will neutralize the grease, and so make them much easier to wash.

Bottles and cruets are cleaned nicely with sand and soapsuds.

Iron pots, stoneware, jars, and crocks should have cold water and a little soda placed in them on the stove and allowed to boil before using them.

Never allow the handled knives to be placed in hot water.

Scrape the dough from your rolling pin and wipe with a dry towel, rather than wash it.

Steel or silver may tarnish in woolen cloths. A chamois skin or tissue paper is very much better.

Don't put your tinware or iron vessels away damp; always dry them first. Scald out your woodenware often.

Don't use a brass kettle for cooking until it is thoroughly cleaned with salt and vinegar.

Don't allow tea or coffee to stand in tin.

Put a lump of camphor in the case with the silverware when packing it away for summer; it will save it from discoloring.

One teaspoonful ammonia to a teacup of water, applied with a rag, will clean silver perfectly.

For cleaning tinware there is nothing better than dry flour applied with a newspaper.

Dissolve a tablespoonful of turpentine in two quarts of hot water and use for washing glass dishes. It gives them a beautiful lustre.

# Practical Points.

Cranberries, if sound in the first place, will keep all the winter in a keg of water. Lemons remain fresh almost indefinitely if covered with cold water which is changed weekly.

To make carpets bright, sprinkle with damp tea-leaves and sweep thoroughly. Draw out grease spots by covering with a coarse brown paper and using a warm flat-iron.

Pumpkin seeds are better than cheese for baiting a mouse-trap.

Apply white of egg with a camel's hair brush to remove specks and soil from gilt frames. Rub with water in which onions have been boiled to removed dust and to brighten the gilding.

Put a thimble over the end of a curtain-rod and the freshly laundered curtains will slip on easily.

An economical cook seldom buys lard. Save all trimmings, skimmings and drippings, place in a saucepan and melt over a moderate fire. Strain into a clean pan and add to each pound of fat a half cup of boiling water and a pinch of soda to sweeten it. Boil slowly until the water is evaporated; strain into a tin pail and keep covered until used.

To remove old putty easily from window frames, pass a red hot poker slowly over it.

To toughen lamp chimneys and glass-ware, immerse in a kettle of cold water to which a tablespoonful of common salt has been added. Boil well, then cool slowly.

In winter use mint vinegar instead of mint sauce with lamb. Wash the leaves well and put into a wide mouthed bottle with good vinegar; keep tightly corked for three weeks, strain into another bottle and cover closely until used.

Clear boiling water will remove fruit and tea stains. Stretch the cloth over a basin and pour the water through the stain, rubbing it gently with a spoon if it seems obstinate.

To take ink out of linen, dip the spot in pure melted tallow; the ink will come out with the tallow in washing.

To kill moths in a carpet without taking it up, wet a thick cloth in water, lay it over the carpet and steam with a hot iron.

Before washing colored stockings let them soak for ten minutes in a quart of cold water containing a tablespoonful of salt. They may then be washed in soap and water without "running."

Puckering of seams in clothing—if the machine tension is not too tight—may be avoided by soaking the spool of thread in water over night and letting it dry before using.

To remove mildew, rub soft or dissolve soap on the spots, scrape chalk on them and lay them in the sun. Repeat if necessary.

# Household Hints.

White of eggs is most nourishing and should be given freely to invalids. Beat slightly and add to tea or coffee, or it may be stirred into any kind of farinaceous food just before serving.

To remove fruit stains from tablecloths, cover with powdered starch and leave this in the stain for a few hours. All the discoloration will then be absorbed by the starch.

When cooking a blanc mange, while yet boiling mix a piece of butter with it, then you will find it turn out of the mold when cold without any trouble, and also that it will have a much glossier appearance.

Cucumber rind, cut into thin strips and put about where ants abound, will invariably drive them away.

An easy way to clean decanters or bottles with small necks is to chop a potato into small pieces. Put these into the decanter with warm water and shake vigorously up and down. When the glass begins to shine, empty out the potato and rinse several times with cold water.

To sweeten jars and tins which have contained tobacco, onions or anything else of strong odor, wash the article clean, then fill it with fresh garden earth, cover it, and let it stand for twenty-four hours. Then wash it and dry it, and it will be quite sweet and fit for use.

If you wish to know whether your coffee is pure sprinkle a small quantity on the surface of a tumbler of water. Pure coffee floats, the adulterated article sinks to the bottom and discolors the water. This is a simple but effective test.

When heating a pie stand it in a deep baking dish filled with boiling water and place on the stove for half an hour, then, twenty minutes before it is required, place it in the oven to heat the crust. It will be as good as if freshly cooked.

In cases of illness, where ice is not procurable for cooling the head of a feverish patient, cut a strip of cucumber, peel rather thick and lay the inner part on the forehead. It is deliciously cool, and remains so for a long time.

To thoroughly clean saucepans after cooking oatmeal, fill them with boiling water, empty away and then fill with cold water, and the oatmeal will almost fall away from the sides of the saucepans.

## HEALTH IN FRUIT AND VEGETABLES.

Water-cress is a remedy for scurvy.
Carrots for those suffering with asthma.
Asparagus induces perspiration and purges the blood.
Spinach is useful for those suffering with gravel.
Lettuce is conducive to sleep.
Blackberries useful in all forms of diarrhea.
Cranberries for erysipelas used internally and externally.
Lemons for feverish thirst in sickness.

## HEALTH AND FOOD.

If the one who makes two blades of grass grow where only one grew before is "a public benefactor," so is the one who improves the daily food of the people, either by supplying articles of superior excellence or by suggesting superior methods of preparation, thus adding to the health and happiness of the people.

This book is presented to the public with the purpose in mind of impressing the importance and suggesting methods of preparing the food that will add to their palatability and wholesomeness.

Your health and that of those dependent upon you, the

pleasures of those who eat at your table, and even economy appeal to you to exercise care and good judgment in buying, so that to be indifferent is almost criminal in these enlightened days.

Health depends in a large degree upon keeping the body well nourished and the system working regularly; if the system becomes clogged, the decaying matter gradually poisons the entire system and headaches, stomach troubles, rheumatism, and almost all other troubles result.

For the proper nourishment of the body pure and palate pleasing food should be prepared, the more pleasing to the eye and palate the more readily the food is digested; the anticipated pleasure of some pleasing looking food starts the flow of saliva and when this is further helped by a savory smell and a palate tickling taste the saliva and the gastric juices make digestion easy.

A very short period of rest puts the system into much better condition for eating. Think deliberately of the house you live in—your body. Make up your mind firmly not to abuse it. Eat nothing that will hurt it. Do not overload it with food that Nature did not intend it to have. Give yourself regular and abundant sleep. This is the only body you will ever have in this world. A pinch of salt in hot water taken just before or just after eating greatly aids digestion and has cured many cases of dyspepsia.

> Eat slow; the rule should surely raise no question
> Unless you'd woo the hag called indigestion —
> The case that taught Napoleon what it cost
> To bolt a meal, in Leipsic's battle lost.

# Terms Used in Cookery.

**A la.** A la mode de, after the style or fashion of.

**Anglaise (á l').** English style. Something plain roasted or plain boiled.

**Aspic.** Savory jelly.

**Au Gratin.** Covered with sauce, breadcrumbs, etc., and browned in the oven or under a salamander.

**Béarnaise.** A word much used in cookery for a rich white herb sauce.

**Béchamel.** French white sauce. Recognized as one of the four foundation sauces. The name of this sauce is supposed to come from the Marquis de Béchamel.

**Bisque.** Name given to certain soups usually made with shellfish.

**Blanc-Mange.** A white sweet food. A sweet cream set in a mould.

**Bouchées.** Small puff-paste patties (petit pâtés), small enough to be a traditional mouthful only.

**Bouillon.** A plain, clear soup. Unclarified beef broth.

**Braisé** or **Braising.** A slow cooking process Meat cooked in a closely covered stew-pan (braising pan or braisière) to prevent evaporation, so that the meat thus cooked retains not only its own juices, but also those of the articles added for flavoring.

**Caramel.** Burnt sugar. A substance made by boiling sugar to a dark brown.

**Charlotte.** Name of a hot or cold sweet dish.

**Compôte.** Usually applied to a delicately prepared dish of stewed fruit, or fruits and jelly.

**Consommé.** Clear, strong gravy soup. The clarified liquor in which meat or poultry has been boiled.

**Croquettes** and **Rissoles.** Names of small, light entrées (prepared with minced meat, etc.)

**Croustades.** Shapes of bread fried, or baked paste crusts, used for serving game, minces, or meats in or upon.

**Croûtons.** Thin slices of bread cut into shapes and fried, used for garnishing dishes and in soups.

**Dessert.** The remains of a meal. Now indicating fruits and sweet=meats served after dinner.

**Éclair.** A French pastry filled with cream.

**Emincé.** Finely sliced or shred.

**Entrée.** A course of dishes, or corner dish for the first course.

**Escalope.** Thin, round steaks of veal, called "collops."

**Espagnole.** A rich brown sauce; the foundation of nearly all brown sauces.

**Filet.** The under cut of a loin of beef, mutton, veal, pork, and game.

**Foie Gras.** Fat goose liver.

**Forcemeat.** Meat for stuffing.

**Fricassée.** A white stew of chicken or veal.

**Fritter, Beignets.** Anything dipped in batter, crumbed, or egged, and fried.

**Gâteau.** A round, flat cake, generally decorated.

**Glacé.** Frozen, iced.

**Gumbo.** The American term for okra soup or other preparations from okra.

**Hors-d'oeuvre.** Appetizers. Dainty relishes, served cold before the soup.

**Liaison.** The mixture of yolk of eggs, cream, etc., used for thickening or binding white soups and sauces.

**Macédoine.** A mixture of various kinds of vegetables or fruits, cut in even-shaped disks.

**Maître d'Hôtel (à la).** Hotel steward's fashion. Also the name of a flavoring butter, mixed with chopped parsley and seasoned with lemon-juice, pepper and salt.

**Mayonnaise.** A cold salad sauce, or dressing.

**Menu.** The bill of fare. Literally the word means minute detail of courses.

**Meringue.** Light pastry, made of white of eggs and sugar, filled with cream or ice.

**Nougat.** Almond rock candy.

**Paprika.** Hungarian red pepper; less pungent than the Spanish pepper.

**Pâté.** A pie; pastry; a savory meat pastry, or a raised pie.

**Potage, Soup.** Broth or liquor; the first course of a dinner.

**Potpourri.** A stew of various kinds of meats and spices.

**Purée.** A smooth pulp; mashed vegetables; thick soups.

**Ragoût.** A rich stew of meat, highly seasoned.

**Relevé.** A course of a dinner, consisting of large joints of meat, game, etc.

**Rémoulade.** A cold sauce, flavored with savory herbs and mustard, used as salad dressing, etc.

**Rôti.** The course of a meal which is served before the entremets.

**Roux.** A preparation of butter and flour, used for thickening soups and sauces.

**Salmi** or **Salmis.** A compôte of game set to finish cooking when half roasted.

**Sauter (ée).** To toss over the fire, in a sauté or frying-pan, in little butter or fat; anything that requires a sharp fire and quick cooking.

**Sorbet.** An iced Turkish drink; also a partly set water ice.

**Soufflé.** Literally "puffed up." A very light baked or steamed pudding, an omelet.

**Soufflé Glacé.** A very light, sweet cream mixture, iced and served in cases.

**Tartare.** A cold sauce, made of yolks of eggs, oil, mustard, capers, gherkins, etc., served with fried fish or cold meats.

**Timbale.** A kind of crusted hash baked in a mould.

**Tutti-Frutti.** A mixture of various kinds of fruits or cooked vegetables.

**Vol-au-vent.** A light, round puff-paste crust, filled with delicately flavored ragoûts of chicken, sweetbread, etc.

# Extracts from the Fish and Game Laws of Massachusetts, 1912

## FISH.

Penalties

**BLACK BASS** not to be taken under 8 inches, or from April 1 to June 20, both dates inclusive . . . . . $10

**PICKEREL** not to be taken under 10 inches, or from March 1 to April 30, both dates inclusive . . . . . $10

**TROUT AND SALMON** may be taken between April 1 and the following July 31, inclusive; **Trout** less than 6 inches in length, not to be taken; **Wild Trout** not to be bought, sold or offered for sale . . . . . . $25

**SMELT** may be taken from June 1 to the following March 14, inclusive, but only with hook and hand line . . . $1

**LOBSTERS,** alive, not to be less than 9 inches; boiled, not to be less than 8¾ inches in length; not to be mutilated; or taken **when bearing eggs** . . . . . $5–100

**FISH which at any time frequent fresh water** may be taken only by artificially or naturally baited hook. Ten hooks may be set or used, provided the hooks are not arranged as a trawl.

**FISH, SPAWN OR ROE** not to be introduced into public waters except by permit from Fish and Game Commission, $50

**EXPLOSIVES AND POISONS** may not be used in fishing waters, or waste materials discharged into streams . . $50

## GAME.

Penalties

All persons must secure from town or city clerk a license for hunting. Fees for unnaturalized foreign-born citizens, $15; non-resident, $10; resident, $1.

**PARTRIDGE, WOODCOCK AND QUAIL** may be taken only on week days from October 12 to following November 12, inclusive. Bag limit: Ruffed grouse, 3 in one day, 15 in one year; quail and woodcock, 4 in one day, 20 in one year . . . . . . . . . . $20

**GRAY OR HUNGARIAN PARTRIDGE** not to be hunted or killed or held in possession . . . . . $50

**PHEASANTS** not to be hunted or killed . . . . $50

**DUCKS, GEESE AND BRANT** may be taken and sold only between September 15 and following December 31, inclusive; on black ducks, bag limit 15 for any one day. **Loons** not to be hunted on fresh water . . . . $20

Penalties

**PLOVER, SNIPE, RAIL AND MARSH OR BEACH BIRDS** may be taken and sold only between August 1 and following December 31, inclusive . . . . . . $20

**HARES AND RABBITS** may be taken between October 15 and following February 28, inclusive . . . . $10

**GRAY SQUIRRELS** may be killed only from October 15 to November 14, inclusive, unless doing damage to buildings or crops; bag limit, 5 in one day or 15 in one year . . $10

**DEER** not to be chased by dogs. Open season to counties of Berkshire, Bristol, Essex, Franklin, Hampden, Hampshire, Middlesex and Worcester, from sunrise of third Monday of November to sunset of following Saturday. Bag limit one deer. Only shotguns to be used . . . $100

**INSECTIVOROUS AND SONG BIRDS** not to be killed, captured or held in possession at any time, or used for millinery purposes . . . . . . . . . $10

**FERRETING, TRAPPING AND SETTING SNARES** prohibited, except that farmers and fruit growers may trap rabbits under permit from Fish and Game Commission, $10–20

**Wood Duck, Swans, Wild Pigeons, Upland Plover, Piping and Killdeer Plover, Herons, Bittern, Eagles, Fish Hawks, Marsh Hawks, Small Owls, Gulls and Terns** not to be killed at any time, or feathers used for millinery purposes, $10–50

**EGGS AND NESTS** of birds protected by law are not to be taken or disturbed . . . . . . . . $10

**SENDING OR CARRYING GAME OUT OF THE STATE** $10–20

**HUNTING on the Lord's day prohibited** . . . . $10–20

**HUNTING, IMPORTING OR LIBERATING Wild Turkeys prohibited** . . . . . . . . . . $20

**PINNATED GROUSE (Heath Hen)** not to be hunted or killed . . . . . . . . . . $100

**Sale of Partridge, Prairie Chicken and Woodcock prohibited, and also after January 1, 1913, of all species of wild birds and game quadrupeds (except Hares and Rabbits) which are protected by law in any part of the United States** . $20

## SALE OF QUAIL KILLED IN THIS STATE PROHIBITED.

# RECIPES FOR SEA FOOD.

## FISH, ETC.

**Baked Fish.** — The best fish to bake are white fish, bass, pickerel, pike, red-snapper, shad, etc., all having white flesh. They should be basted often and a stuffing also serves to keep the fish moist as well as to season it.

Clean, wipe and dry the fish. If the fish is slimy, like a muskalonge, scald with hot water before attempting to clean. Rub with salt inside and out, stuff and sew with soft darning cotton, leaving a large knot at one end that you can find after the fish is baked; cut gashes two inches apart on each side so they will alternate — not opposite each other — and skewer into the shape of an S or O; put the fish on a sheet, rub all over with soft butter, salt and pepper, and place narrow strips of salt pork in the gashes; dredge with flour (or not, just as you please), and put into a hot oven without water; baste with hot water and butter as soon as it begins to brown and repeat every ten minutes afterwards. Remove it carefully from the fish sheet and place it on a hot platter, draw out the string, wipe off all the water or fat which runs from the fish and remove the pieces of pork. Pour Hollandaise sauce around (not over) the fish, or serve a drawn butter sauce flavored with lemon, and pile Saratoga chips lightly around the fish. Garnish the head of the fish with parsley or water-cresses. Fish that have been frozen are almost sure to break; if they do, fill the broken places with parsley.

**Broiled Fish, No. 1.** — Large fish should be split through the back to broil and for most stoves the head and tail must be removed. Use a double wire broiler and grease it well before laying in the fish. Dust the fish with salt and pepper and broil the flesh side first till almost done, then cook on the skin side just long enough to brown it well. Small fish require from five to ten minutes. Thick ones from fifteen to twenty minutes. Turn a dripping pan over the broiler and it will cook more evenly. There is no excuse for scorching the fish, as one can always scatter a few ashes over a hot fire. Spread generously with butter and set in the warming oven a minute to let it penetrate the fish. Garnish with parsley or water-cress after taking from the oven.

**Broiled Fish, No. 2.** — Clean, wash, and wipe dry. Split so that when laid flat the backbone will be in the middle, or take the backbone out. Sprinkle with salt and lay, inside down, upon a buttered gridiron over a clear fire until it is nicely colored, then turn. When done, put upon a hot dish, butter plentifully, and pepper. Put a hot cover over it and send to table.

**Fried Fish.** — Fish for frying should be thoroughly dried after cleaning, seasoned with salt and pepper, rolled in fine bread crumbs, dipped in beaten egg, rolled in crumbs again, fried in deep fat like doughnuts; put in only a few pieces at a time to avoid chilling the fat and let it reheat before frying any more. The temperature should not fall below 375 degrees. From two to five minutes is sufficient for any but extra large pieces. The fish is done when it rises to the top of the fat. Drain perfectly, dry on paper and arrange on a folded napkin. Fry the parsley that is to garnish the dish, taking care to have it crisp, without changing its color.

**Panned Fish.** — This is suitable for any small fish or such as can be cut in slices. Have the fish well cleaned, seasoned with pepper and salt and dried with a little flour or, better still, very fine bread crumbs. Have a large frying-pan smoking hot with as little grease in it as will keep the fish from sticking. Dripping from good, sweet salt pork is the best, but any sweet dripping will do. When the fat begins to smoke blue lay in the fish and brown quickly on both sides, then cover closely and set back to cook more slowly, from ten to twenty minutes, according to size of the fish. Bass in all its varieties is suitable to cook in this way, so are butter-fish, cisco, perch, herring, trout, bream, etc.

**Steamed Fish.** — Clean carefully, but without removing head or fins. Rub inside and out with salt, pepper, and lemon juice, laying slices of onion inside, if liked. Lay on a buttered paper and steam till the flesh parts easily from the bones. Lay on a folded napkin, dress with lemon and parsley and send to the table with Poulette sauce.

**Fish Broth.** — Fry four ounces of butter with the following vegetables sliced fine : two onions, two carrots, and two leeks. Fry until quite dry. Then add four pounds of fish, — such as bass, black fish, flounder, or any bony fish, — the head of a fresh cod, one quart of white wine, and six quarts of water. Season with salt, peppercorns, bunch of parsley, and a few blades of mace. Cover the stew-pan and boil one-half hour. Strain the broth and free it from its fat. Chop up two pounds of cod or bass, mix with two eggs, add the broth and a few more sliced vegetables. Set on the fire and stir constantly until it begins to boil. Then let it simmer for ten minutes and strain through a wet cloth. Pour in a tureen with three or four dozen veal forcemeat balls fried in hot lard.

**Baked Bass.** — Wash and clean a fresh bass for baking, leaving on the head. Stuff the fish with the following mixture : two and one-half cups of fine bread crumbs, one cup of butter, the rind of a quarter of a lemon chopped very fine, two or three sprigs of parsley chopped fine, and a little sweet marjoram. Season to taste with salt and white pepper. Mix two well-beaten eggs with a little water, and add to the mixture. When the fish is well stuffed, sew up the opening. Score it on each side, in the spaces place very thin slices of salt pork. Place it in a pan with a little stock, and bake in a moderate oven. When thoroughly cooked, carefully place it on a hot dish.

To the gravy which is left in the pan, add a little tomato sauce. Stir on the top of the range until it comes to a boil. Strain and serve in a separate dish. Garnish the fish plate with parsley and thin slices of lemon.

**Palmettes of Striped Bass.** — Cut out six heart-shaped fillets from the thickest part of the bass. Season with pepper, salt, and the juice of half a lemon. Put under a press for one-half hour. Cook in clarified butter for ten minutes until a delicate brown. Make a forcemeat (the same as for fillet of pampano). Color the forcemeat pink and green, also have some white. Pour in three pastry bags. On the outside of each palmette put a pink border, on the inside all white with a small heart shape of green on the top. Set them away to get chilled. Have six pieces of heart-shaped oiled paper. Wrap up each palmette in one. Place them in a tin pan, set the pan over another which is half filled with water. Cook in the oven until the forcemeat is done, or from twenty to twenty-five minutes. Serve on corn-starch croustade and with Hollandaise sauce.

**Boiled Bass, or other Fish.** — Put sufficient water in pot to enable fish, if alive, to swim easily. Add one-half cup vinegar, one teaspoonful salt, one onion, one dozen whole black peppers, one blade mace. Sew up fish in piece of clean net or muslin, fitted to shape. Heat slowly for first one-half hour; then boil eight minutes.

**Baked Bluefish.** — Select a nice large bluefish, clean, and prepare it for baking. Wash it in salted water, and after drying it thoroughly, stuff with veal forcemeat for fish, or else with bread forcemeat, to which a few capers have been added. Sew up the opening and rub the fish all over with salt. Then having put small pieces of butter over it, place it in a large pan with enough water to cover the bottom, and bake in a hot oven for forty-five or fifty minutes. After it begins to bake, sprinkle it with a little salt and pepper. Baste it often with the liquid in the pan, and a little melted butter. When it is cooked and a nice color, remove carefully to a hot plate. Do not break it. Serve with a brown sauce, or any desired sauce poured round the fish as a garnish, or serve it in a separate dish.

**Broiled Bluefish, Anchovy Butter.** — Procure a three-pound piece fresh bluefish, trim off fins and remove all bones. Mix on a plate a tablespoonful oil, teaspoonful salt, and one-half teaspoonful pepper, turn bluefish in this seasoning six or more times, then arrange on a broiler and broil for six minutes on each side. Remove to a hot serving dish, spread anchovy butter over it, decorate with a little green parsley and slices of lemon.

**Fried Bluefish, and other Kinds.** — Clean, wipe dry, inside and out. Sprinkle with flour, and season with salt. Fry in hot butter or sweet lard. One-half lard and one-half butter make a good mixture for frying fish. The moment fish are done to good brown, take them from fat and drain in hot strainer; garnish with parsley.

**Bluefish, Sweet-pepper Butter.** — Remove bones, neatly wipe a three-pound fresh bluefish; season all over with teaspoonful salt, half teaspoonful pepper; rub all over with tablespoonful oil, then broil on brisk fire for six minutes on each side. Dress on hot dish, spread sweet-pepper butter over surface and keep dish at oven door ten minutes, basting fish with butter once in a while. Remove, decorate with a little parsley and six quarters lemon, and serve.

**Corn-starch Croustade.** — Place one pint of milk in a saucepan over the fire, and when it boils add two heaping table-spoonfuls of corn-starch, which has been dissolved in a little cold water, and one-half teaspoonful salt. When the mixture has cooked five minutes, add the white of an egg. Wet a mould about three-fourths of an inch deep of the desired shape and pour in the mixture. While hot it may be colored pink or green. Set away to cool.

**Fried Cod or Haddock.** — Remove the skin (ask the fish-dealer to remove it for you), cut in square pieces and remove the backbone. Scrape all the fish from the bones, and press it with a knife into the larger pieces. Season with salt and pepper and roll in fine white corn meal. Fry several slices of salt pork, enough to have a cup of fat. Lay the fish in the hot fat, cook brown on each side. Drain on soft paper and serve hot. Spread with butter, and garnish with slices of lemon.

Any fish having firm white flesh can be prepared in this manner and it is a vast improvement on the old method of sending all the bones to the table.

**Baked Cod.** — Select a fresh cod, cut off the head and fins, draw, wash, and split it down the belly. Remove the bone from the thick part only, and make small lengthwise incisions in the skin in order to prevent the fish from curling while it is cooking. Put it to soak for three hours in a dressing made as follows: Salt, white pepper, a little Worcestershire sauce, and some sweet oil. Drain and place in a pan. Baste it with melted butter and sprinkle with fine bread crumbs. Moisten with two glasses of white wine and one pint of oyster liquor. Bake in a slow oven and then cover with a buttered paper and bake a light brown in a moderate oven. Drain and thicken the liquid with a little flour kneaded with butter, add some lemon juice and finely chopped parsley. Pour this round the fish and serve.

**Small Fish Baked.** — Lay in a baking dish with chopped onion, mushrooms and parsley, rub the fish with salt, pepper, a bit of nutmeg and dot with butter. Pour in enough thin broth to cover bottom of dish, add the juice of one-half lemon and bake till the flesh parts easily from the bone.

**Baked Cod's Head.** — Wash and thoroughly clean a cod's head. Stuff the gills with veal forcemeat. Place the head in a pan, season with salt, white pepper, and a little chopped parsley. Mix one pint of stock, a scant pint of Sherry wine, and a little tomato catsup, and pour into the pan. Cover the fish with buttered paper and bake in a moderate oven. The fish must be well basted while it is cooking. When the head is nearly cooked, sprinkle it with fine bread crumbs. The average-sized head should bake in one hour and a quarter. Mix the liquor in the pan with two gills of brown sauce, strain it, and add two ounces of butter and a little lemon juice. Boil for four minutes and then pour over the fish or serve in separate dish.

**Stuffing for Baked Fish, No. 1.** — For a fish weighing four to six pounds take one cup of cracker crumbs, one saltspoonful of salt, one saltspoonful of pepper, one teaspoonful of chopped onions, one teaspoonful of chopped parsley, one teaspoonful of capers, one teaspoonful of chopped pickles.

**Bread Stuffing for Fish, No. 2.** — Take about half a pound of stale bread and soak in water, and when soft press out the water; add a very little chopped suet, pepper, salt, a large tablespoonful of onion minced and fried, and, if prepared, a little minced parsley; cook a trifle, and after removing from the fire add a beaten egg.

**Bread Stuffing, No. 3.** — Bread crumbs with a little chopped parsley and pork, salt, pepper and butter. Fill up the fish, sew it closely, then bake.

**Boiled Cod with Oysters, No. 1.** — Put the fish into boiling water, slightly salted; add a few white cloves and peppers and a bit of lemon-peel; pull gently on the fins, and when they come out easily the fish is done. Arrange neatly on a folded napkin, garnish, and serve with oyster sauce. Take six oysters to every pound of fish and scald (blanch) them in a half-pint of hot oyster liquor; take out the oysters and add to the liquor salt, pepper, a bit of mace and an ounce of butter; whip into it a gill of milk containing a quarter of a tablespoonful of flour. Simmer a moment, add the oysters, and send to table in a sauce-boat.

**Boiled Cod, No. 2.** — Take the head and shoulders of a good-sized cod. Scrape and wash clean ; rub a handful of salt into it ; flour a cloth and pin the fish in it. Put into boiling water, and boil half an hour. Take the fish carefully from the cloth, and serve with egg sauce. Potato is the only vegetable that is nice with boiled cod.

**Codfish Fritters.** — Cut codfish into strips size of the finger. Freshen over night in cold water. In morning wipe dry, dip each piece in fritter batter and fry a nice brown in hot fat.

**Broiled Cod, or Scrod.** — Split, wash, and wipe dry a small cod. Rub the gridiron with a piece of fat pork, and lay the fish upon it, being careful to have the inside downward. If the fish is very thick cook thirty minutes ; but for an ordinary one, twenty minutes will be sufficient. Have the dish in which you intend serving it warm ; place it upon the fish and turn the dish and gridiron over simultaneously. If the fish sticks to the gridiron loosen it gently with a knife. Have some butter warm, but *not melted*, with which to season it. Shake on a little pepper and salt and send to the table.

**Codfish Balls, No. 1.** — Boil one cup codfish with four good-sized potatoes ; when done mash potatoes and fish together, add good-sized piece of butter, a little pepper and one egg beaten ; roll in a little flour to form balls and place in frying-pan ; fry brown on one side in butter, turn and brown the other side.

**Codfish Balls, No. 2.** — Put fish in cold water, set on back of stove ; when water gets hot, pour off and put on cold again until fish is fresh enough ; then pick it apart. Boil potatoes and mash them ; mix fish and potatoes together while potatoes are hot, taking two-thirds potatoes and one-third fish. Put in plenty of butter ; make into balls and fry in plenty of lard. Have lard hot before putting in balls.

Variation may be had by rolling each ball in beaten egg, then in dry bread crumbs before frying.

**Codfish Balls, No. 3.** — Trim and soak a piece of salt codfish in cold water for six or seven hours, and during that time change the water two or three times. Shred it. Should it be too salt after shredding, freshen it by frequent changes of cold water. There should be one quart bowl of the shredded fish.

Cover it with water and let it simmer gently until tender. It will not take very long. Should you boil it too much, you might harden it. Have ready six good-sized, fresh-boiled potatoes, and mash them while hot. Have the fish drained, pounded, and rubbed through a sieve, and mix with the three well-beaten eggs. Season to taste with salt — if necessary — and white pepper, also a small lump of butter. Drop by the tablespoonful into a pan of boiling hot lard and fry until a delicate brown. Drain on brown paper and serve very hot.

**Fish Balls, No. 4.** — Take the fish left from the dinner, put it in your chopping tray, being careful that there are no bones in it; chop fine. Pare and boil potatoes enough to have twice the quantity of potatoes that you have of fish. When cooked turn them into the tray with the fish, mash fine, and make into balls about the size of an egg. Flour the outside lightly; have the fat boiling hot, and fry a light brown. The fat should be half lard and half salt pork. Have the slices of pork a nice brown, and serve with the fish balls.

**Fish Balls, No. 5.** — Two cupfuls cold boiled codfish, fresh or salted. Chop the fish when you have freed it of bones and skin; work in one cupful of mashed potatoes, and moisten with a half cup of drawn butter with an egg beaten in. Season to taste. Have them soft enough to mold, yet firm enough to keep in shape. Roll the balls in flour, and fry quickly to a golden brown in lard or clean dripping. Take from the fat as soon as they are done; lay in a colander or sieve and shake gently, to free them from every drop of grease. Turn out for a moment on white paper to absorb any lingering drops, and serve on a hot dish.

**Dropped Fish Balls, No. 6.** — One-half pint of raw fish, one heaping pint of pared potatoes (let the potatoes be under medium size), two eggs, butter the size of an egg and a little pepper. Cut the fish in half-inch slices across the grain, and measure it lightly. Put the potatoes into the boiler and the fish on top of them; then cover with boiling water and boil half an hour, or until tender. Drain off all the water and mash fish and potatoes together until fine and light. Then add the butter and pepper and the eggs, well beaten. Have a deep kettle of boiling fat. Dip a tablespoon in it and then take up a spoonful of the mixture, having care to get it into as good shape as possible. Drop into the boiling fat and cook until brown, which should be in two minutes. Be careful not to crowd the balls and also that the fat is hot enough. The spoon should be dipped in the fat every time you take a spoonful of the mixture. These balls are delicious.

**Fish Cakes.** — Wash salt codfish and separate in pieces; there should be one cupful. Wash, pare and soak potatoes and cut in pieces of uniform size; there should be two cupfuls (heaping). Put fish and potatoes in kettle with a generous supply of boiling water, and cook until potatoes are soft. Drain, return to kettle, mash, add one egg, well beaten, one teaspoonful butter, one-eighth teaspoonful pepper, and a few drops of onion juice. Shape in flat cakes, roll in flour and sauté in pork fat.

**Canapes of Meat or Fish.** — Toast six pieces of bread and cut them in good-sized squares. Beat the whites of four eggs to a stiff froth, put them in a pastry bag, and then make a border round each piece of toast. Bake in quick oven till light brown. Fill in the centre with creamed fish or finely minced creamed meat and serve very hot.

**Fish Chowder, No. 1.** — Take a fresh haddock, of three or four pounds, clean it well, and cut in pieces of three inches square. Place in the bottom of your dinner-pot five or six slices of salt pork, fry brown, then add three onions sliced thin, and fry those brown. Remove the kettle from the fire, and place on the onions and pork a layer of fish. Sprinkle over a little pepper and salt, then a layer of pared and sliced potatoes, a layer of fish and potatoes, till the fish is used up. Cover with water, and let it boil for half an hour. Pound six biscuits or crackers fine as meal, and pour into the pot; and, lastly, add a pint of milk; let it scald well, and serve.

**Fish Chowder, No. 2.** — Four pounds of fish, half cod and half haddock, if you can get the two kinds, two onions, six potatoes, eight white browns, one quarter of a pound of salt pork, salt, pepper. Prepare the chowder as directed in the preceding rule; split the crackers and lay on the top, pour over the whole hot water enough to cover, and boil fifteen minutes; then wet two tablespoonfuls of flour with one-third of a cup of cream. Stir this into the boiling chowder, let it boil up once, and serve.

When you cannot get the white browns, pilot bread will answer. When a very strong flavor of onions is desired, use four onions.

**Fish Chowder, No. 3.**—Take either a cod or haddock, skin it, loosen the skin about the head, and draw it down towards the tail, when it will peel off easily. Then run your knife down the back close to the bone, which you take out. Cut your fish in small pieces and wash in cold water. Put the head on to boil in about two quarts of water, and boil twenty minutes. For a fish weighing six pounds, pare and slice *thin* five good-sized potatoes and one onion. Place a layer of potatoes and onion in the pot, then a layer of fish, dredge in a little salt, pepper, and flour. Keep putting in alternate layers of potatoes and fish until all used. Use about one tablespoonful of salt, one teaspoonful of pepper, one teacup of flour, in all.

Have ready half a pound of salt pork fried brown. Pour this over the mixture; add about two quarts of cold water, then strain on the water in which the head has been boiled. If this is not water enough to cover, add more cold. Cover tight, and boil gently thirty minutes. If not seasoned enough, add what you please. When it has boiled twenty minutes, put in six crackers which have been soaked three minutes in cold water. If you wish to add milk and butter, you can do so about five minutes before taking it up.

**Fish Chowder, No. 4.** — Skin a four-pound haddock, wash thoroughly, and cut the flesh from the bones in pieces about two inches square. Cover the head and bones with cold water and boil one-half hour. Slice two small white onions in a pan with four slices of thin, fat, salt pork. When tender, skim out the pork and onions and add the strained bone liquor and one quart of sliced raw potato. Cook for ten minutes, then add the fish, one tablespoonful of salt, and one-half teaspoonful of white pepper. When the potatoes are tender, add one quart of hot milk which has been thickened with two ounces of butter and flour mixed together. Do not break the fish by needless stirring. Split six butter crackers, arrange in a tureen, and pour the fish chowder over them.

**Fish Chowder, No. 5.** — Cut two or three slices of salt pork into dice pieces; fry to crisp, and turn the whole into chowder kettle. Pare six medium-sized potatoes and cut them in two. Peel small onion and chop fine. Put potatoes into kettle with part of onion.  Cut fish (which should be fresh cod or haddock) into convenient pieces, and lay over potatoes ; sprinkle over it rest of the onion.  Season well with salt and pepper, add just enough water to come to top of fish.  Pour over the whole quart can tomatoes ; cover closely and allow to cook about as long as takes to boil potatoes ; then add two quarts milk, and let it scald up again.  Season with tomato catsup, and more salt and pepper if required.

**Cape Ann Fish Chowder.** — This is the everyday style of fish chowder among the fishermen's families : Wash and cut in chunks two pounds of fresh cod or haddock.  Pare and thinly slice one quart of potatoes (or as many as you prefer) and place in cold water until you are ready for them.  Cut two slices of fat salt pork in dice and slowly fry out in chowder kettle until fat is extracted, stirring often.  Remove scraps, add one large onion sliced, and fry slowly for a very few minutes.  Then in your kettle place a layer of fish and one of potatoes, salt and pepper, and continue that way until all is used, potatoes on top.  Cover with cold water and let come to boil, then boil slowly or simmer, until potatoes are done.  Mix one tablespoonful flour with one of butter, add to chowder with one pint milk.  Allow to come to boiling point once more, add a few halved crackers and serve very hot.  Cheap and delicious.

**New England Chowder.** — Take a good haddock, cod, or any other solid fish, cut it in pieces three inches square ; put a pound of fat salt pork, cut into strips, into the pot ; set it on hot coals and fry out the grease ; take out the pork, but leave the grease in the bottom of the pot, and put in a layer of fish, over that a layer of sliced onions, over that a layer of fish, with slips of fried pork, then another layer of onions and a few sliced raw potatoes, and so on alternately until your fish is all in ; mix some flour with as much water as will fill the pot ; season to suit your taste, and boil for half an hour ; have ready some pilot bread, soaked in water, and throw them into your chowder five minutes before taking off ; serve in a tureen.

**Colonial Codfish Pie, with Crust.** — Line a deep baking dish with a biscuit crust.  To make the crust, sift together four cups of flour, one heaping teaspoonful of soda, and two teaspoonfuls of cream of tartar (or in place of these three heaping teaspoonfuls of baking powder), and one teaspoonful of salt.

In this rub one-half cup of shortening and about a pint of milk, that is, enough to make a medium soft dough. In rolling out the crust spread butter on twice and fold and roll out.

Take a pint of picked-up salt codfish, cover it with boiling water, let it stand two minutes and drain. Pour on more water, and, after it has stood, drain dry. Upon the crust of your baking dish put a layer of this codfish, sprinkle it with bread crumbs, pepper (a little salt if you find the fish fresh), small pieces of butter, and some cream sauce (made by thickening one pint of boiling milk with two teaspoonfuls of flour and seasoning with salt and pepper). Break over the fish, bread crumbs and seasoning three or four eggs, carefully preserving the yolks. Repeat these layers, codfish, bread crumbs, cream sauce, and eggs, put on the top crust, cut a few holes in the centre to let out the steam, and bake till the crust is a delicate brown.

**Creamed Fish.** — Steam two pounds codfish, break in flakes, removing bones and skin. Make one pint white sauce (see Meat and Fish Sauces). Grease a baking dish, fill with alternate layers of fish and sauce, seasoning with salt, pepper, chopped parsley, and lemon juice or a few drops of vinegar. Mix together one cup dry bread crumbs and three tablespoonfuls melted butter; spread over top and brown in quick oven.

This may be varied by using tomato, bechamel, curry, or any other sauce, or by adding grated cheese or sliced hard-boiled eggs to the white sauce; by baking in shells or patty-pans in place of the deep dish, or by covering with mashed potato or biscuit crust instead of crumbs.

**Fish Loaf.** — Three pounds haddock. Have head, tail, skin and backbone removed, so you have two slices of solid fish. You can use cod, but I like haddock better. On the bottom of your baking pan put three slices fat pork. On this place one layer of the fish, sprinkle with salt and pepper. Mix one cup soft bread crumbs, little salt, pepper and one-quarter cup melted butter, pork fat or bacon fat and spread over the fish slice. Cover with the other slice of fish, sprinkle with salt and pepper and place three or four slices of fat pork on top. Bake about thirty minutes. Just before it is done remove pork, scatter one-half cup cracker crumbs over fish, replace pork and brown in oven, serve with drawn butter sauce, to which you add a hard-boiled egg or a white sauce. If you haven't milk enough for the white sauce use milk and water.

**Fish Balls.** — Take one pound boneless codfish, set on stove in cold water (after picking it into small pieces), let it come to a boil, then remove, and if it is too salty do it over the same way. Boil potatoes and mash them. Take less potato than fish. Cut up a lot of all-fat pork into tiny dice shape and fry out crisp and brown. Put fish through a fine cutter or the meat grinder, beat one egg light and mix all together. Season with pepper. Mix in the pork scraps, too, and if they are not moist enough to hold together in balls add two tablespoonfuls of the pork fat. Fry in the fat left from scraps till a golden brown. Make cakes or balls about an inch thick when molded.

**Fish Croquettes.** — Put one large tablespoonful of butter in a saucepan. Let it bubble, then put in a little onion cut in small pieces, then a large spoonful of flour and some salt and pepper, then put in your fish and beat it up, then put the yolk of an egg in and beat it up. Put away to cool. When cool form into cone shape and roll in cracker crumbs again and fry in hot fat. They are nice. You can use chicken instead of fish.

**Curried Cod.** — Two slices large cod, or remains of any codfish, three ounces butter, one onion sliced, a teacup of white stock, thickening of butter and flour, one tablespoonful of curry powder, one-quarter pint of cream, salt and cayenne to taste. Flake the fish and fry to a nice brown, color with the butter and onions; put this in a stewpan, add the stock and thickening, simmer for ten minutes. Stir the curry powder into the cream; put it with the seasoning into the other ingredients; give one boil and serve. Time, three-quarters of an hour. Sufficient for four persons.

**Fish Cutlets.** — Cut the fish in squares or in slices across the back, removing all the bones. Dry, dip in batter and fry in deep boiling lard. It is quite necessary that the lard should boil. When a gold color, drain till dry on brown paper and serve on a folded napkin with a quantity of parsley or cresses and a thin slice of lemon. A tomato, mayonnaise, or tartare sauce may be served with cutlets.

**Fish Hash.** — Prepare the fish as for fish balls; chop fine cold potatoes, and mix with the fish. Fry brown six good slices of salt pork; take out the pork and turn the hash into the frying-pan; add half a cup of boiling water; let this heat slowly, stirring often; then spread smoothly, and brown, being careful not to let it burn. When brown, fold it as you would an omelet, dish, and garnish the dish with the slices of pork. When the pork is objected to, butter can be used instead.

Salt fish, when cooked and chopped, will keep for a week if nothing else is mixed with it. When intending to have hash or fish balls for breakfast, the fish should be chopped the night before, and the potatoes should be pared and put in cold water. Put the potatoes on the fire as soon as it begins to burn. They will then be ready for use when you are ready for them.

**Fish with Green Pepper.** — One and three-quarters cups cold cooked fish, one cup white sauce, one-half small green pepper, one-half slice onion or flavor to taste with extract onion. Salt and pepper.

Cut a slice from stem end of pepper, remove every seed and parboil pepper fifteen minutes. Make a white sauce with one cup milk, two tablespoonfuls butter, two tablespoonfuls flour, bit of bay leaf, sprig of parsley, salt and pepper to taste, scalding the milk with the parsley and bay leaf, cook the onion finely chopped in the butter three minutes, or flavor with onion extract to taste; add the flour when well mingled, the milk, salt, and pepper; when thickened and smooth add the fish broken into flakes and the green pepper cut into narrow strips; heat thoroughly, and serve with brown bread sandwiches.

This is easily prepared in the chafing-dish, having the green pepper previously cooked.

**Fish au Gratin.** — Six pounds of any fish with white meat, steamed, freed from skin and bone and broken into flakes. One pint of cream sauce and one cup cracker crumbs moistened with melted butter; put a layer of fish in a gratin dish, season well with salt, pepper, cayenne, and celery salt, and sprinkle with chopped parsley, pour over a part of the cream sauce, repeat till the fish is all used, reserving most of the sauce to pour over the top; sprinkle buttered crumbs over the top and bake in a rather quick oven till it boils up in the middle and the crumbs are brown.

**Codfish a la Mode.** — Take one teacup of salt codfish picked up fine, two teacups of mashed potatoes, one pint of cream or milk. Mix them well together and then add two eggs well beaten. Stir them in thoroughly and then add a half cup of butter, and salt and pepper to taste. Put in a baking dish and bake twenty or thirty minutes.

**Maigre Fish Pie.** — Have ready plenty of salt codfish boiled and free from bones and skin. Have ready also four hard-boiled eggs and four onions. Peel and slice the eggs and onions very thin. Line the bottom of a deep pie dish with fish forcemeat or a layer of boiled potatoes sliced thin. On this put a layer of onions, then a layer of fish, then of eggs, and so on till the dish is full. Season each layer with a little pepper, and pour over the layers a gill of water containing a teaspoonful of made mustard, a teaspoonful of the essence of anchovy, and a little mushroom cat-sup. Break in small bits over the top an ounce of fresh butter. Cover all with a puff paste and bake an hour. For this dish fresh fish may be used by adding a little salt.

**A Norwegian Fish-Pudding.** — Take a five or six pound haddock, clean, skin, fillet and scrape to a pulp with a knife. Pound in a mortar until it is smooth; add one teaspoonful salt and one tablespoonful butter, and continue working for ten minutes. Transfer to a large bowl and work in with a potato masher two egg yolks blended with one cup of cream, putting it in by spoonfuls; add another cup cream and one-half pepper-spoonful allspice. Beat furiously and when it is frothy put in a buttered mold and steam for three hours. If desired, the top may be browned before serving, but it should be done quickly. Serve with cream and caper sauce. It should be fine, smooth and firm as blanc mange. Fresh cod may be used instead of haddock. Instead of making a pudding the paste may be formed into balls the size of an egg, steamed in a close mold or box and afterwards fried brown in butter and served either with or without sauce, or they may be poached in curry sauce or made very small and dropped into a thick fish soup. In frying fish Norwegian cooks often dust the pieces with grated cheese and add a little to the sauce served with the fish.

**Slices of Cod a la Seville.** — Wash and dry one-half pound of Carolina rice, fry it in hot olive oil, drain on a sieve, and then put it in a stew-pan with some pieces of fresh cod in pieces about four inches square, and which have been fried in olive oil and drained. Cut a Spanish onion in very thin slices, and also fry the slices in oil. Mix them with six ripe tomatoes from which the skins and seeds have been removed. Cook the onion and tomato slowly for five minutes, then pour it over the fish and rice. Season with a little cayenne, salt, and lemon juice. Moisten with one pint of white broth, place a buttered paper on top, cover with the lid of the pan, and place in the oven to bake. In about half an hour the fish and rice will be done. Remove the pieces of fish and with a wooden spoon stir the rice over the fire in order to mix it with the seasoning. Arrange the rice on a dish and place the pieces of codfish on it. Garnish with tomato sauce or mussel sauce.

**Shredded Cod baked with Cream Sauce.** — Boil four or five pounds of fresh cod. When cooked, drain and shred in fine pieces and set away to cool. Make the following sauce for a five-pound piece of fish : Boil one quart of milk with one onion and a little finely chopped parsley. Set it aside. Mix one cup of butter with enough flour to absorb it. Add this to the milk and boil until it is the consistency of custard. Season with a dash of cayenne and salt to taste. Put a layer of shredded fish in a baking dish, cover with a layer of sauce, then a layer of fish and so on until the dish is filled. Have the last layer of cream. Cover with fine bread crumbs. Sprinkle with pieces of butter and bake in the oven until the top is a nice brown. Small boiled potato balls covered with cream sauce should be served with this.

**Fish Forcemeat, No. 1.** — Take two ounces of fish free from skin, put in a mortar with two ounces of fresh butter, one ounce of bread crumbs, the yolks of two eggs boiled hard, and a little shallot, grated lemon peel, and minced parsley. Pound together till quite smooth, mix with salt, pepper, and the yolk and white of an egg, and it is ready for use.

**Fish Forcemeat, No. 2.** — Take one pound of raw fish, — halibut, cod, pompano. Mortar it well and put it through a puree sieve. Weigh it ; there should be four ounces, good weight. Then add the beaten white of one egg. Set in a cool place. Melt one tablespoonful of butter with one of flour. When they come to a boil, add one cup milk, the yolk of one egg, one tablespoonful cream. Season to taste. Cook until it thickens and is smooth, remove, and when cold add to your fish.

**Veal Forcemeat for Fish.** — Soak four ounces of stale bread in water, squeeze it dry, and mix with four ounces of finely chopped cooked veal and two ounces of finely chopped salt pork and one tablespoonful of butter. Pound all in a mortar, then rub through a puree sieve, and add the following: the juice of half a lemon, half a teaspoonful of powdered thyme, half a teaspoonful of sweet marjoram, a little ground mace, a little salt and white pepper and a well-beaten egg. This may be made in larger or smaller quantities, according to the size and number of the fish to be stuffed.

**Fish Toast.** — One cup flaked cold fish, free from skin and bones. Heat in water sufficient to moisten; add butter, pepper and salt. When hot pour on slices of buttered toast; garnish with eggs poached in muffin rings.

**Baked Haddock.** — Clean a four-pound haddock. Sprinkle with salt inside and stuff and sew. Cut gashes on each side of backbone and insert narrow strips of salt pork. Place on a greased fish sheet or something to raise it from the bottom. Sprinkle with salt and pepper, dredge with flour, and place around fish small pieces of salt pork. Bake one hour in a hot oven, basting often. Serve with drawn butter sauce or egg sauce.

**Finnan Haddie.** — Soak fish in milk and water to cover, using equal parts, one and one-half hours on back of range. Drain, separate into flakes and rinse thoroughly in warm water. There should be two cupfuls. Cook one-quarter cup butter with one tablespoonful of finely-chopped onion five minutes, add quarter cup flour, one cup each of milk and cream, one-half teaspoonful of paprika, one and one-half teaspoonfuls of salt, and when mixture thickens add the flaked fish and one-third cup canned red peppers, cut in strips. Cover bottom of dish with cooked macaroni, pour over the fish and set in oven for five minutes; then sprinkle grated cheese over top and put under gas flame to remain until cheese is melted.

To vary this, use a cup of potatoes cut in cubes and mix with the fish, omitting the macaroni.

**Savory Finnan Haddie.** — Soak finnan haddie in milk to cover one hour. Bake thirty minutes and separate into flakes; there should be two cups. Cook one-half tablespoonful finely chopped onion and three and one-half tablespoonfuls finely chopped green peppers in one-quarter cup butter five minutes, stirring constantly. Add one teaspoonful salt, one-half teaspoonful paprika and a few grains pepper and cook three minutes; then add four tablespoonfuls flour and stir until well blended. Pour on gradually, while stirring constantly, one cup each milk and cream. Bring to the boiling point and add finnan haddie. Turn into a buttered dish, cover with buttered crumbs and bake until the crumbs are brown.

**Finnan Haddies.** — *To Broil:* First heat broiler and grease well to keep from sticking; then place meat side to the fire and cook slowly fifteen minutes; careful not to burn. Butter and pepper to suit taste; garnish with slices of lemon or parsley.

*To Bake:* Place fish in cold water, then place on fire and let it come to a boil; then remove skin and place in a pan with two or three slices of fat pork; bake in a moderate oven twenty-five or thirty minutes.

*To Boil:* Place fish in boiling water and boil for twenty minutes; serve with egg sauce or drawn butter.

*Smoked Haddies in Cream:* Tear haddies into small strips; wash clean and place in basin with quart of water; let it simmer half an hour, then pour off water and add one pint of fresh milk. When this comes to a boil, thicken with one spoonful of flour, let it boil five minutes and add butter (size of a walnut) and a little pepper and serve.

*Drawn Butter:* Beat one cup of butter and two spoonfuls of flour to a cream; pour over this one pint of boiling water; set on fire and let it come to a boil, *but do not boil.* Serve immediately.

*Egg Sauce:* Chop up two hard boiled eggs and stir into drawn butter.

**Fried Catfish.** — Catfish must be cooked quite fresh — if possible, directly out of the water. The larger ones are generally coarse and strong; the small-sized fish are the best. Wash and clean them, cut off their heads and tails, remove the upper part of the backbone near the shoulders, and score them along the back with deep gashes or incisions. Dredge them with flour, and fry them in plenty of lard, boiling fast when the catfish are put into the pan. Or you may fry them in the drippings of gravy saved from roast beef or veal. They are very nice dipped in a batter of beaten egg and grated bread crumbs, or they may be done plain, though not in so nice a way, with Indian meal instead of bread crumbs. Drain off the lard before you dish them. Touch each incision or cut very slightly with a little cayenne before they go to table.

DRYING FISH

**A Salt Codfish Dish.** — Remove the skin and cut in pieces two and one-half pounds of salt cod. Soak for eighteen hours in cold water, changing water two or three times. Drain, place fish in a saucepan with cold water to cover it and let cook slowly (but not boil) for twenty minutes. Drain and remove all bones, place cod in a saucepan; then squeeze in the juice of a lemon and add drop by drop half a gill of olive oil, sharply stirring while adding it. Then pour in also, little by little, a half gill of cream, a teaspoonful of chopped parsley, one salt-spoonful of cayenne and mix well. Serve on a hot, deep dish with slices of toasted bread around.

**Fried Eels, No. 1.** — After skinning, emptying, and washing them as clean as possible, cut them into short pieces, and dry them well with a soft cloth. Season them with fine salt and cayenne, flour them thickly, and fry them in boiling lard; when nicely browned, drain and dry them, and send to the table with plain melted butter and a lemon, or with fish sauce. Eels are sometimes dipped into batter and then fried, or into egg and dried bread crumbs, and served with plenty of crisped parsley.

**Eels Fried in Batter, No. 2.** — Cut a large eel weighing about two pounds in quite thick slices. See that it is clean. Place in a basin with a little salt and pepper and some vinegar. Let the pieces soak for several hours. They must be turned occasionally. Drain thoroughly, then dip in batter and fry in hot fat. When a nice brown, drain on paper and serve very hot with a brown or tomato sauce.

**Baked Eels.** — Prepare as for frying; then put into a baking pan with a little water, flour, pepper, and salt. Bake twenty minutes. Make a gravy of the liquor in which they were baked, adding a little butter.

**Baked Eels with Tartare Sauce.** — Skin two fat eels, each weighing about one and a half pounds. Cut off the fins, heads, and tails. Clean them thoroughly and tie them together so as to shape them on a round platter. Wrap them in a wet cloth and cook slowly in court bouillon for fifteen minutes. Set aside and let them cool in the liquor. Season about one pint of fine bread crumbs with one teaspoonful of salt, one saltspoonful of pepper. Carefully remove the cloth from the fish, wipe dry, and cover them with the bread crumbs. Then spread them with a mixture of two well-beaten eggs and one tablespoonful of olive oil. Sprinkle once more with bread crumbs. Place them in a baking pan, being particular to keep the circular shape. Add two and a half tablespoonfuls of butter. Bake in moderate oven for half an hour. Baste them three times. Place on a circular dish. In the centre place green peppers filled with tartare sauce after you have removed the core and seeds from peppers, soaked them in cold water, drained thoroughly, and then filled them with the sauce.

**Frog Legs.** — The green marsh frogs furnish the best hams, as they are more tender and have less of the strong muddy flavor. They are generally liked fried. Pare off the feet and truss them by inserting the stump along the shin of the other leg. Put them, with salt, pepper, and lemon juice to steep for an hour, then drain and roll in flour, then in beaten egg, and in fine bread crumbs. Fry to a light brown in hot fat. Serve with fried parsley.

**Frog Legs a la Mariniere.** — Saute three dozen legs with two ounces of butter, one-half pint chopped mushrooms, four shallots. As soon as well-colored add a tablespoonful flour, a little salt, pepper, and cayenne, and moisten with a half pint of white wine and enough consomme to nearly cover. Boil ten minutes. Mix the yolks of four eggs with two tablespoonfuls cream and stir it into the boiling mixture. Remove at once from the fire and serve.

**Stewed Frogs a la Poulette.** — Trim, truss, and marinate as for frying. Cook in a sautoir with two tablespoonfuls butter, salt, pepper, and speck of nutmeg. Cook briskly and long enough to evaporate the water without allowing them to burn. Add two glasses white wine, a pint of velvet sauce; cover and boil till quite tender. Skim, add a liaison of four egg yolks, one tablespoonful chopped parsley, the juice of a lemon and two ounces of butter. Mix well and serve with fried croutons.

**Baked Cod or Halibut.** — Use a piece of fish from the middle of the back weighing four, five, or six pounds. Lay the fish in very cold salt-and-water for two hours; wipe dry; make deep gashes in both sides at right angles with the backbone, and rub into these, as well as coat it all over with, a forcemeat made of crumbs, pork, herbs, onion, and seasoning, made to adhere by raw egg. Lay in the baking pan and pour over it the drawn butter (which should be quite thin), season with the anchovy sauce, lemon juice, pepper, and a pinch of parsley. Bake in a moderate oven nearly an hour, or even more if the piece be large — basting frequently lest it should brown too fast. Add a little butter-and-water when the sauce thickens too much. When the fish is done, remove to a hot dish, and strain the gravy over it. A few capers or chopped green pickles are a pleasant addition to the gravy.

**Baked Halibut, No. 1.** — Arrange six thin slices of fat salt pork (about two and one-half inches square) in a baking pan. Wipe a two-pound (or as much as you happen to have) piece of halibut with a damp cloth and place it in the pan. Mask the fish with three tablespoonfuls of butter creamed and mixed with three tablespoonfuls of flour; then cover the top with three-quarters of a cupful of buttered cracker crumbs and arrange five thin strips of fat salt pork over the crumbs. Cover with buttered paper and bake fifty minutes in a moderate oven, removing the paper during the last fifteen minutes to brown the crumbs and pork. Garnish with thin slices of lemon (cut in fancy shapes if desired) then sprinkle with finely chopped parsley. Serve with the following sauce: Melt three tablespoonfuls of butter, add three tablespoonfuls of flour; stir until well blended, then pour on gradually, while stirring constantly, one and one-half cups of hot water. Bring to the boiling point; add three tablespoonfuls of butter and season with one-half teaspoonful of salt and one-eighth teaspoonful of pepper.

**Baked Halibut, No. 2.** — Cut about two pounds of halibut into pieces two inches square, clean and wipe dry and put in a dish with four wineglassfuls of Sherry wine, turning them from time to time and let remain in the wine two hours. Then put the pieces of fish into a baking pan, moisten well with melted butter, sprinkle lightly with bread crumbs and let bake until done and nicely browned. Take up the fish and pour into pan in which it was baked half a pint of cream. Heat on top of stove, thicken with a little flour, pour over fish and send to table garnished with parsley. Or if preferred melt a little more butter in pan, add a little lemon juice to it and pour over fish. If the wine is not objectionable you will find this delicious and half the portion sufficient for two.

**Boiled Halibut.** — Take a small halibut, or what you require from a large fish. Put it into the fish kettle, with the back of the fish undermost ; cover it with cold water, in which a handful of salt and a bit of saltpetre the size of a hazel-nut have been dissolved. When it begins to boil skim it carefully, and then let it just simmer till it is done. Four pounds of fish will require half an hour nearly to boil it. Drain it, garnish with horse-radish or parsley. Egg sauce, or plain melted butter, are served with it.

**Broiled Halibut, No. 1.** — Season the slices with salt and pepper and lay them in melted butter for half an hour, having them well covered on both sides. Roll in flour and broil for ten minutes over a clear fire. Serve on a hot dish, garnishing with parsley and slices of lemon. The slices of halibut should be about an inch thick and for every pound there should be three tablespoonfuls of butter.

**Broiled Halibut, No. 2.** — Slices of halibut, salt, pepper, butter. Cut the slices of fish about an inch thick, season with pepper and salt, and lay them in melted butter one-half hour, allowing three tablespoonfuls of butter to a pound of fish, then roll them in flour, and broil about twenty minutes. Serve very hot.

**Broiled Halibut with Maître d'Hôtel Butter, No. 1.** — Butter both sides of the broiler. Season the slices of halibut with salt and pepper, place them in the broiler and cook over clear coals for twelve minutes, turning frequently. Place on a hot dish and spread on them the sauce, using one spoonful to each pound. Garnish with parsley.

**Halibut, Maître d'Hôtel, No. 2.** — Cut three pounds of halibut into pieces three inches square. Dip each in beaten egg, then in sifted bread crumbs. Fry in boiling lard to a rich brown. Rub a heaping teaspoonful of butter to a cream, add the juice of a lemon, a tablespoonful of chopped parsley, salt and pepper, mix and spread on the hot squares of halibut, set in the oven just long enough to melt, then serve. Not difficult, and delicious for summer breakfasts.

**Fried Halibut.** — Let the slices lie in cold salted water, to which has been added one cup of vinegar, for ten or fifteen minutes. Dry them afterwards thoroughly by wiping with a towel, and dusting cracker meal on both sides. Lay them in smoking hot salad oil, and they will be well cooked and of a pale brown in three or five minutes, according to thickness of the slices.

### Baked Chicken Halibut — Hollandaise Sauce. — Clean
a slice of halibut, brush over with melted butter, and sprinkle with salt, pepper, and onion juice. Put in baking pan, cover with paper, and bake fifteen minutes. Serve with Hollandaise sauce.

*Hollandaise Sauce :* Put one-half tablespoonful vinegar and the yolks of two eggs in a saucepan; set in a larger pan of boiling water. Stir quickly with a wire spoon, adding gradually three-quarters cupful butter (the salt having been removed by washing). When sauce is thickened, remove from the fire, and add a few grains cayenne and salt.

### Halibut Cutlets. — Cut your halibut steaks an inch thick,
wipe them with a dry cloth, and season with salt and cayenne pepper. Have ready a pan of yolk of eggs well beaten and a dish of grated bread crumbs. Put some fresh lard or beef drippings in a frying-pan and hold it over the fire till it boils. Dip your cutlets in the egg, and then in the bread crumbs. Fry a light brown; serve up hot. Salmon or any large fish may be fried in the same manner.

### Fried Fillets of Halibut. — Remove the skin and bones
from a slice of halibut weighing one and one-quarter pounds. Cut each of the four pieces thus made, in halves lengthwise, making eight fillets. Sprinkle with salt, pepper, and lemon juice. Roll and fasten with small wooden skewers. Dip in crumbs, egg, and crumbs, and fry in deep fat.

### Halibut Rabbit. — Melt one teaspoonful butter, add a few
drops of onion juice and one tablespoonful corn-starch mixed with one-half teaspoonful salt and one-quarter teaspoonful paprika, then pour on gradually one cup milk, add three-quarters cup of soft cheese, cut fine, and one cup of cold, flaked, cooked halibut. When cheese is melted add one egg slightly beaten and one tablespoonful lemon juice. Serve on crackers.

### Scalloped Halibut. — Shred one cupful of cold boiled hali-
but ; pour in the food pan one and one-half cups milk and let come

to a boil; add butter size of an egg, salt and pepper, then the crumbs of four crackers, add lastly the halibut; let it cook five minutes, then add two hard-boiled eggs chopped fine, and serve on a hot platter with bits of buttered toast.

**Halibut Salad.** — Steam a slice of halibut, first well rubbed over with salt, until the flesh easily separates from the bone; remove skin and bone and with a fork separate it into flakes into attractive pieces, not mincing it too fine to have a leftover appearance, add a seasoning of salt, and French dressing to which has been added a few gratings of raw onion. When ready to serve pour off what French dressing has not been absorbed and arrange in a salad dish with alternate layers of fish, cold boiled peas, cucumbers cut in cubes and sprinkled with salt and salad cream. Garnish with heart leaves of lettuce and serve with any kind of sweet pickle or with spiced gooseberry.

**Halibut Salad with Cucumber Spirals.** — Halibut salad is an appetizing, warm weather dish for luncheon or Sunday night's supper. Steam a slice of halibut three inches thick. Its flavor is improved if a soup bunch is thrown into the steamer with it. It is done when tender enough to remove the skin and bone, which should be accomplished while it is still hot without disturbing the shape. Pour over it a French dressing made of four tablespoonfuls of olive oil, two of vinegar, with salt and pepper to taste. When cold, arrange on a bed of lettuce hearts and fill the cavity from which the bone was taken with the best of them.

The dish is prettily garnished with curls, spirals, or cups of cucumber, made as follows: Cut a cucumber crosswise in sections three-quarters of an inch thick. Cut each section round and round in one long, thin paring. Mayonnaise dressing fills these cups, or is served with the fish in a separate sauce cup if the cucumbers are served in the usual way, that is, sliced with a French dressing.

**Herring Salad.** — Soak over night three Holland herrings, cut in small pieces. Cook and peel eight medium potatoes and when cold chop with two small cooked red beets, two onions, a few sour apples, some roasted veal, three hard-boiled eggs; mix with a sauce of sweet-oil, vinegar, stock, pepper and mustard to taste. A tablespoonful of thick, sour cream is an improvement to the sauce, which should stand over night in an earthen dish.

**Fresh Mackerel Boiled.** — If not cleaned, open them at the gills, take out the insides, wash clean, and pin in a fish-cloth. (Do not use the cloth that you use to boil mackerel for any other fish.) Drop into boiling water, and boil fifteen minutes. Serve with drawn butter.

**Broiled Mackerel.** — Split down the back and clean. Be careful to scrape all the thin black skin from the inside. Wipe dry and lay on the gridiron ; broil on one side a nice brown, then turn and brown the other side ; it will not take so long to brown the side on which the skin is. (All fish should have the side on which the skin is turned to the fire last, as the skin burns easily and coals are not so hot after you have used them ten minutes.) Season with butter, pepper and salt.

**Fried Mackerel.** — Fry brown six good-sized slices of pork. Prepare your mackerel as for broiling. Take out your pork, sprinkle a little salt over the mackerel, then fry a nice brown. Serve the fried pork with it.

**Baked Mackerel, No. 1.** — Prepare as for boiling. Make a dressing as for baked cod. Stuff with this, dredge with salt and flour. Bake thirty minutes, basting often with water, butter and flour. Make a gravy with the water in the pan in which the fish is baked. Always make the gravy quite salt. The best way to cook mackerel is to *broil* it.

**Baked Mackerel, No. 2.** — Split and clean two small mackerel. Place in a buttered dripping pan, sprinkle with salt and pepper, and pour over one-half cupful thin cream. Bake in hot oven twenty minutes.

**Baked Mackerel, No. 3.** — Split fish, clean and remove head and tail. Put in buttered dripping pan and sprinkle with salt and pepper and dot over with butter (allowing one tablespoonful to a medium-sized fish), and pour over two-thirds cup milk. Bake twenty-five minutes in hot oven.

**Salt Mackerel.** — Soak salt mackerel about forty-eight hours, changing the water once, then put it in a pan, cover with cream or the richest milk. Put in the oven and cook until cream is brown.

**To Boil Salt Mackerel.** — Wash the mackerel, and soak over night in clear cold water. Put them on to boil in cold water, and boil gently thirty minutes. Serve with drawn butter.

**To Broil and Fry Salt Mackerel.** — Soak over night and cook the same as fresh.

**Salt Mackerel in Cream.** — Freshen as for broiled mackerel, then lay into a baking pan, and to one mackerel add half a pint of new milk, put into the oven, and bake twenty-five minutes. About five minutes before it is dished, add a small piece of butter. This is a nice dish for breakfast and dinner.

**Broiled Salt Mackerel.** — Freshen by soaking it overnight in water, taking care that the skin lies uppermost. In the morning dry it without breaking, cut off the head and tip of the tail, place it between the bars of a buttered fish-gridiron, and broil to a light brown; lay it on a hot dish, and dress with a little butter, pepper, and lemon juice, vinegar, or chopped pickle.

**Planked Fish.** — Purchase a wooden plank one and one-half by one foot. Butter the plank quite freely, then lay on slices of cod, halibut, or whole fish, cover with thin strips of pork, then put in roasting pan and bake. When done, make pyramids of mashed potatoes around it, return to oven and brown. Put plank on large platter and serve. Garnish with thin slices of tomatoes.

**Fried Perch.** — Scale and clean them perfectly; dry them well, flour and fry them in boiling lard. Serve plenty of fried parsley round them.

**Fish or Meat Ramekins.** — A delicious luncheon dish or an entree for dinner may be made from leftover fish or meat. Cut the meat or fish very fine, but do not grind it. Add a well-beaten egg, a little milk and a few bread crumbs. Season well with salt and pepper. Put a piece of butter the size of a walnut in each ramekin and then add the mixture and bake until brown.

**Boiled Rockfish.** — After the fish has been nicely cleaned, put it into a pot with water enough to cover it, and throw in salt in the proportion of half a teaspoonful to a pound of fish. Boil it slowly until the meat is tender and easily separates from the bones. A large fish will require an hour to cook. When done, serve on a hot dish, and have a few hard-boiled eggs, cut in thin slices, laid around it and over it. Eat with egg sauce.

**Fried Roe.** — Wash and wipe, fry twenty minutes in hot fat in a frying-pan, turning at the end of fifteen minutes. Season, dish on a hot platter and garnish with fried oysters or fried potatoes. Garnish with a great bunch of parsley at each end and a half lemon set in the parsley.

**Scalloped Fish, No. 1.** — Two cups cold fish (cod, haddock or halibut), one and one-half cups milk, one slice onion, blade of mace, bit of bay leaf, three tablespoonfuls butter, three tablespoonfuls flour, one-half teaspoonful salt, one-eighth teaspoonful pepper, one-half cup buttered crumbs.

Scald the milk with onion, mace, and bay leaf. Remove seasonings. Melt the butter, add flour, salt and pepper, then gradually the milk. Boil three minutes. Put one-half the fish in a buttered baking dish, sprinkle with salt and pepper and pour over one-half the sauce. Repeat, cover with buttered crumbs and bake until the crumbs are brown in a hot oven.

**Scalloped Fish, No. 2.** — Skin and cut into small pieces a cod or haddock, and lay in a deep earthen dish. Dredge in about half a cup of flour, one spoonful of salt, one teaspoonful of pepper. Cut about two spoonfuls of butter into small pieces and strew in; cover the whole with new milk and bake forty minutes.

**Stewed Fish with Oysters.** — Cut the fish in pieces for serving, remove the skin and bone. Spread a thick coating of butter over the bottom of the stew-pan, lay in the fish, season each layer with salt and pepper, pour on boiling water to more than cover, add a tablespoonful of lemon juice or vinegar and simmer fifteen or twenty minutes, or till the fish is cooked but not broken. Add a tablespoonful of flour cooked in a tablespoonful of hot butter, mix it well with the boiling liquid without breaking the fish. Add a quart of oysters, or enough to equal the fish. Simmer until the oysters are plump. Add more seasoning if needed and serve very hot.

**Spiced Fish.** — Steep six cloves, six allspice kernels, six peppercorns, and one tablespoonful of brown sugar in one cup of sharp vinegar and boil ten minutes; pour it over one pint of cold flaked fish.

**Broiled Scrod.** — Scrod is one of two famous Boston importations; the other is broiled lobster. Scrod is young cod, and one may weigh from two and a half to five pounds; the best weigh four or five pounds. When thoroughly broiled it should be rich, flaky, and delicious. Rub the gridiron with fat pork and broil the inside of the fish first. Twenty minutes is usually sufficient to broil a fish of ordinary size. Serve with warmed butter, pepper, and salt.

**Baked Salmon with Cream Sauce.** — Butter a sheet of foolscap paper on both sides, and wrap the fish up in it, pinning the ends securely together. Lay in the baking pan, and pour six or seven spoonfuls of butter-and-water over it. Turn another pan over all, and steam in a moderate oven from three-quarters of an hour to an hour, lifting the cover, from time to time, to baste and assure yourself that the paper is not burning. Meanwhile, have ready in a saucepan a cup of cream, in which you would do well to dissolve a bit of soda a little larger than a pea. This is a wise precaution whenever cream is to be boiled. Heat this in a vessel placed within another of hot water; thicken with a heaping teaspoonful of corn-starch; add a tablespoonful of butter, pepper, and salt to taste, a liberal pinch of minced parsley, and when the fish is unwrapped and dished, pour half the dressing slowly over it, sending the rest to table in a boat. If you have no cream use milk, and add a beaten egg to the thickening.

**Baked Salmon, No. 1.** — Clean the fish, rinse it, wipe it dry; rub it well outside and in with a mixture of pepper and salt, and fill it with a stuffing made of slices of bread, buttered freely and moistened with hot milk or water (add sage or thyme to the seasoning if liked); tie a thread around the fish, so as to keep the stuffing in (take off the thread before serving); lay muffin rings, or a trivet in a dripping pan, lay bits of butter over the fish, dredge flour over, and put it on the rings, put a pint of hot water in the pan to baste with; bake one hour, if a large fish, in a quick oven; baste frequently. When the fish is taken up, having cut a lemon in very thin slices, put them in the pan, and burn it.

**Baked Salmon, No. 2.** — Take four salmon steaks weighing one pound each. Place in a buttered saucepan with one pint white wine, one pint white broth, white pepper, salt, a little grated nutmeg, a bunch of parsley with a few whole spices or herbs wrapped in it, and two ounces of butter. Let it come to a boil, then cover and simmer for one-half hour. Drain the fish and remove the bunch of parsley. Thicken the liquid with one ounce of flour which has been cooked in butter. Boil ten minutes, then mix with the yolks of four eggs and some chopped parsley. Spread a thin layer of thick mashed potatoes in an oval baking dish, well buttered. Remove the bone and skin from the steaks and place them one overlapping the other on the potatoes. Fill with more potatoes, smooth nicely, and pour the sauce over all. Sprinkle with bread crumbs and little pieces of butter over the top. Bake until a light brown, in a moderate oven, about twenty minutes. Serve in the baking dish.

**Boiled Salmon.** — A piece weighing six pounds should be rubbed with salt, tied carefully in a cloth, and boiled slowly for three-quarters of an hour. It should be eaten with egg or caper sauce. If any remain after dinner it may be placed in a deep dish, a little salt sprinkled over, and a teacupful of boiling vinegar poured over it. Cover it closely and it will make a nice breakfast dish.

**Salmon, Boiled Plain.** — Have ready a fish kettle with enough boiling soft water to cover the fish; wash off the water from the fish and let it come rather slowly to the boil again. Simmer very gently till done, allowing about fifteen minutes to each pound. Throw in one tablespoonful salt just before it is done. Serve with plain drawn butter sauce.

**Broiled Salmon, No. 1.** — Select as many slices of salmon as required. Sprinkle with a little chopped parsley and mixed herbs, salt and pepper, and some olive oil. Let the slices soak for one hour, turning occasionally so the fish will absorb the seasoning. Arrange on a well-greased gridiron and broil over a clear fire. Baste occasionally with the oil seasoning which is left. When nicely browned and thoroughly cooked, place on a hot dish, and garnish with parsley and slices of lemon. Serve a white sauce in a separate dish.

**Broiled Salmon, No. 2.** — The steaks from the centre of the fish are best. Sprinkle with salt and pepper, spread on a little butter, and broil over a clear but slow fire.

**Salmon Bone Broiled.** — In filleting a fish to be broiled, leave a half-inch or more of meat on the backbone. Rub well with salt and cayenne pepper and broil over a clear fire till well browned. This is delicious for breakfast.

**Salmon and Rice.** — Form freshly boiled rice into flat cakes, brown slightly in butter on both sides and place on a warmed platter. Warm a can of salmon and dip over the rice. Over this pour a white sauce into which has been stirred the whites of two hard boiled eggs cut in dice. Garnish with the yolks cut into slices.

**Salmon Croquettes.** — One can salmon, one-half cup of milk, one tablespoonful of flour, one egg; come to a boil until thick; a little lemon juice; roll in crumbs and fry in hot lard.

**Canape of Smoked Salmon.** — Cut out from a stale loaf of whole wheat bread six slices one-quarter of an inch thick, then cut each into two-inch square pieces. Toast them to a nice golden brown and lightly butter; cover them with very thin slices of smoked salmon, nicely trim, dress on a side dish with a folded napkin, decorate with a little parsley, six quarters of lemon and a hard boiled egg finely chopped; sprinkle this over them and serve.

**Salmon Cutlets.** — Cut two or three pounds of cold boiled salmon in very small pieces. Mix some boiled lobster coral and half an ounce of butter, pound in a mortar, and rub through a hair sieve. Place one gill of milk in a saucepan with one ounce of butter and one ounce of flour which have been creamed together. Stir over the fire until it becomes thick and does not stick to the sides of the pan. Then stir in the salmon, coral, a dash of cayenne pepper, salt, and lemon juice to taste. Remove from the fire. When cold, shape the mixture into cutlets, brush them with beaten egg, roll in fine bread crumbs, and fry until a nice brown in hot fat. Drain on hot paper. Serve on a hot dish garnished with fried parsley. Serve lobster sauce separately.

**Salmon Steaks or Cutlets Fried.** — Cut slices from the middle of the fish one inch thick; wipe dry and salt slightly; dip in egg, then in cracker crumbs; fry very quickly in hot butter; drain off every drop of grease, and serve upon a hot dish. Sprinkle green parsley in bunches over it. The French use the best salad oil in this recipe instead of butter.

**Darne of Salmon.** — If the middle cut; there are but two or sometimes three from a large fish. Lay in a stew-pan on a bed of sliced carrots and onions (two tablespoonfuls each), parsley and peppercorns; dredge lightly with salt and pour over one pint claret, one pint thin broth, dot with three tablespoonfuls butter and cover with a buttered paper. Bring quickly to a boil and simmer very gently one hour. Drain and remove the skin, mask with a Remoulade sauce. The liquor in which the fish is cooked can be strained and used several times.

**Fillets of Salmon a la Venitienne.** — Take the fillets from a four-pound tail-piece of salmon. Remove the skin and cut each one in four long pieces. Flatten and trim evenly. Fasten fine strips of larding pork on one side, season with salt, white pepper, and a little lemon juice, and place the larded side up in a buttered pan. Moisten with half a pint of white wine, and cover with a sheet of buttered paper with a small hole in the centre. The steam must have vent, else the surface will not glaze. Cook in the oven about forty minutes, basting frequently with the liquid in order to have the glaze a nice color. Drain and dish the fillets in a circle with alternate heart-shaped slices of bread fried in butter. Thicken two ladlefuls of broth with an ounce of flour kneaded in butter. Stir and boil a few minutes. Add two ounces of butter, a little lemon juice, and chopped parsley. Mix well and pour in centre of dish.

**Salmon Mousse a la Martinot.** — Have a slice of raw salmon, scrape so it will be free from sinews, put it in a mortar and pound to a pulp, and put through a fine puree sieve. Then weigh it. There should be eight ounces, good weight. Place in a bowl and gradually add the beaten whites of two eggs, stirring constantly with a wooden pestle. Make a sauce of the following: One tablespoonful of melted butter, one tablespoonful flour. Let them come to a boil. Add one cupful milk, two tablespoonfuls of mushroom liquor, one-half teaspoonful of salt, one-fourth teaspoonful of white pepper, a pinch of cayenne, and juice of one onion. Cook all together five minutes, add the yolks of three eggs and two tablespoonfuls of cream. Do not let the sauce boil after the yolks have been added. When the sauce commences to thicken, remove and set away to cool. When cold, add it to the fish. Rub all well together and put on ice for half an hour. Then add half a pint of whipped cream. Butter your mold, decorate it with truffles. Put on ice to harden, so the decoration will be firm on mold. Fill the mold with fish, giving it a few knocks on the table to settle the forcemeat. Thirty minutes before serving put your mold in a pan, pour hot water halfway to mold, put a buttered paper on top, and poach in a moderate oven until firm to the touch. When ready to serve, dip your mold in cold water, lay the dish you are going to serve it in on top of mold. Turn very gently and lift off the mold. Serve with Martinot sauce in centre or in sauce-boat.

**Salmon or Meat Omelet.** — A very little left-over salmon or meat chopped fine will make a fine dish for breakfast. For four persons beat slightly four eggs, add one cup of milk, one-quarter teaspoonful salt, one tablespoonful flour (mixed together), and meat or salmon. In an ordinary spider place good-sized piece of butter. When very hot turn in mixture, cover tightly and brown.

**Fish Salad.** — Shred some boiled salmon, halibut, or other fish, mix with it half as much boiled potato cut in small cubes; serve on lettuce leaves with salad cream. Shredded lettuce or peas may be used in place of potatoes. Garnish with sliced lemon and boiled beets cut in fancy shapes.

**Salmon Sandwiches.** — Take a nice solid piece of boiled salmon, mince it very fine, and season to taste with pepper, salt, and a little Worcestershire sauce. Mix all into a paste with melted butter. Make a highly seasoned French dressing of vinegar, oil, pepper and salt, and pour over cucumbers which have been peeled and sliced very thin. Then set them on the ice for fifteen or twenty minutes. Evenly spread two thin slices of unbuttered bread with the salmon mixture. Put a slice of cucumber between them and shape sandwich according to the general rule. You may prepare your bread spread with salmon one-half or three-quarters of an hour before serving, but the cucumbers should be added at the last moment. Canned salmon may be used. If it is, use the butter sparingly.

**Smoked Salmon, Broiled.** — Take a half pound of smoked salmon and parboil it ten minutes; lay in cold water for the same length of time; wipe dry and broil over a clear fire. Add two tablespoonfuls of butter while hot; season with cayenne and the juice of half a lemon; pile in a "log-cabin" square upon a hot plate, and serve with dry toast.

**Pickled Salmon.** — Soak salt salmon twenty-four hours, changing the water frequently; afterward pour boiling water around it, and let it stand fifteen minutes; drain off and then pour on boiling vinegar with cloves and mace added.

**To Cook Salt Codfish.** — The fish should be thoroughly washed and soaked in cold water twelve hours. Change the water and put on to cook. As soon as the water comes to a boiling point, set back where it will keep hot, but will not boil. From four to six hours will cook a very dry, hard fish, and there are kinds which will cook in half an hour. If it has hung in a furnace heated cellar till hard, it will never come tender. It is best not to buy more than will be used in a week or two. Like ham, bacon and meat in general, it should be hung, not laid on a shelf.

**Soaking Salt Fish.** — Very salt fish should be soaked several hours in three or four changes of warm water. Place the skin side up, so that salt crystals may fall away from the under or meat side. Wipe carefully and clean, then soak for an hour in very cold water.

**Salt Fish Dinner.** — Soak a pound of salt fish in cold water. When time comes put your potatoes on to boil for dinner. Peel them first. Cut up one pound salt mixed pork in tiny squares and fry a nice brown. When potatoes are about half done put on your salt fish and cover with water. Boil fifteen minutes. Drain fish and put on platter. Put the pork scraps in a gravy boat and potatoes in a covered dish. Mix your potato and fish together on your plate at dinner and have the pork scraps for gravy. Serve with tomato sauce, johnnycake, and pickles.

**Broiled Salt Fish.** — Cut a square the size you desire from the thickest part of the fish. Take off the skin, and wash clean; broil over clear coals ten minutes, then dip in boiling water, butter and serve. This is a nice relish for breakfast or tea, and with boiled potatoes makes an excellent dinner.

**Creamed Salt Codfish.** — Garnished with Hard-boiled Eggs. — Pick in small pieces one cup salt codfish; cover with lukewarm water and let stand on back of range until softened. Melt one tablespoonful butter, add one tablespoonful flour, and pour on gradually one cup hot milk. Add fish, and turn on a hot platter. Garnish with slices of hard-boiled eggs. Serve with baked potatoes.

**Salt Fish in Cream.** — Tear a piece of fish into small strips, wash clean, and place it in a basin with about a quart of water; let it simmer half an hour. Then pour off the water, and add one pint of new milk. When this comes to a boil, thicken with one spoonful of flour, let it boil five minutes, then add butter the size of a walnut and a little pepper, and serve.

**Cleaning a Shad.** — Scale and scrape it carefully; split it down the back and remove the contents, reserving the roe or melt. Wash well and cook as desired.

**Planked Shad, No. 1.** — Have a hardwood board about one inch and a half thick. Split the shad as for broiling, tack it on the board, skin side down, and roast before the fire until done. Every once in a while rub it with a little butter. Before placing the shad on the board, see that the board is well seasoned and heated, else the fish will have the flavor of the wood. When cooked, place in a hot dish, season with salt and pepper, cover with small bits of butter, and serve with lemon cut in quarters.

**Planked Shad, No. 2.** — Split and clean a small shad. Put skin-side down on an oak plank, one inch thick. Sprinkle with salt and pepper, and brush over with melted butter. Bake twenty-five minutes in a hot oven. Spread with butter, and garnish with lemon cut in fancy shapes and parsley. Send to table on plank.

**Broiled Shad.** — Scrape, split, wash, and dry the shad on a cloth; season with pepper and salt; grease the gridiron well; as soon as it is hot lay the shad on to broil with the inside downward. One side being well browned, turn it. It should broil a quarter of an hour or more, according to the thickness. Butter well and send to table hot.

**Broiled Shad à l'Abbé with Herb Sauce.** — Get one large roe shad and an extra shad roe. Prepare the fish for broiling, taking the roe and keeping it with the other until wanted. Remove the bone of the fish, clean nicely, wash and wipe dry. Make small incisions on both sides of the fish and soak it for one hour in a dish with salt, pepper, olive oil, and lemon juice. See that it soaks on both sides. Drain, sprinkle with bread crumbs, and broil slowly for one-half hour. See that your broiler is well greased. Make eight pieces out of your roe and also have eight large oysters. Dip them in beaten egg and roll in bread crumbs and fry in hot fat until a nice brown. Dish up the shad, surround with roes and oysters, and serve with an herb sauce.

**Baked Shad.** — Many people are of the opinion that the very best method of cooking a shad is to bake it. Stuff it with bread crumbs, salt, pepper, butter, and parsley, and mix this up with beaten yolk of egg; fill the fish with it, and sew it up or fasten a string around it. Pour over it a little water and some butter, and bake as you would a fowl. A shad will require from an hour to an hour and a quarter to bake.

**Roast Shad with Sauce.** — Have a large roe shad, scale, draw by the gills, cleanse nicely, and wipe dry. Make small crosswise incisions on both sides. Put the fish on a dish to soak for one hour with salt, pepper, olive oil, lemon juice, chopped parsley, chives, and thyme. Be sure to turn and press it often so it will absorb the seasoning. Put on the spit or on a long skewer, if to roast in the oven, wrap in double oiled paper, making it secure by pressing down a shorter skewer along each side and tying at each end. Then roast before the fire, or in a moderate oven for forty minutes. Remove the paper, brown a nice color. Place on dish, pour sauce round it, and serve.

**Baked Shad Roe.** — Pare the roes of four large shad, sprinkle a baking dish with chopped onions, parsley, and mushrooms. Add the roes, strew over them more onion, etc., with salt, pepper, a little nutmeg, and small bits of butter. Moisten with a little white broth and two glasses of white wine. Let all cook and boil in the oven, basting occasionally, for twenty minutes. Drain and thicken the liquid with one tablespoonful of flour kneaded in butter. Pour this over the roes, sprinkle with fine bread crumbs, put small bits of butter on top, and bake in brisk oven ten minutes longer. Press lemon juice over and serve in the baking dish. The above is enough for eight persons.

**Shad Roe Cromeskies.** — Wash thoroughly in cold water the roe of a shad and remove the skin hanging to it. Wipe it well and cut it in pieces of a size to wrap well in thin slices of bacon. Rub the pieces of shad with salt and pepper. Lay them in the slices of bacon, wrap the bacon round, and tie with fine twine. Have care that the bacon is not too thick. Drop each piece in deep hot fat and fry a light brown. Garnish with parsley and serve with a piquant sauce.

**Pickled Shad or Bluefish.** — Put the fish on the drainer or sheet in the kettle, add one tablespoonful of salt for each quart of water and enough boiling water to just cover the fish; cook slowly until the flesh separates from the bone, thirty minutes or less. Drain and let cool. Cut the flesh in pieces. To half the water in which the fish was cooked add pickling spice, a tablespoonful to a quart, and simmer half an hour or more. Add as much cider vinegar as liquor, and heat and pour over the fish, taking care that the liquor covers the contents. The pickle will be ready for use in one or two days and will keep in a cool place about ten days.

**Smelts.** — The only way to cook smelts is to fry them, although they are sometimes baked. Open them at the gills. Draw each smelt separately between your finger and thumb, beginning at the tail; this will press the insides out. (Some persons never take out the insides, but it should be done as much as in any other fish.) Wash them clean, and let them drain in a colander; then salt and roll in a mixture half flour and half Indian meal. Have about two inches deep of boiling fat in the frying-pan (drippings if you have them; if not lard); into this drop the smelts, and fry brown. Do not put so many in that they will be crowded; if you do, they will not be crisp and brown.

**Smelts as a Garnish.** — Smelts fried plain or rolled in meal or flour and then fried are often used to garnish other kinds of fish. With baked fish they are arranged around the dish in any form that the taste of the cook may dictate; but in garnishing fish or any other dish, the arrangement should always be simple, so as not to make the matter of serving any harder than if the dish were not garnished. Smelts are also seasoned well with salt and pepper, dipped in butter and afterwards in flour and placed in a very hot oven for eight or ten minutes to get a handsome brown. They are then served as a garnish, or on slices of buttered toast. When smelts are used as a garnish, serve one on each plate with the other fish. If you wish to have the smelts in rings for a garnish, fasten the tails in the opening at the gills with little wooden toothpicks; then dip them in the beaten egg and in the crumbs, place in the frying basket and plunge in the boiling fat. When they are cooked take out the skewers and they will retain their shape.

**Baked Smelts.** — Line a well-buttered flat baking dish with forcemeat and arrange the smelts on it. Sprinkle with finely chopped parsley and mushrooms, season with salt, pepper, and a little grated nutmeg. Cover with veloute sauce, which has one glass of white wine mixed with it. Then sprinkle with bread crumbs, and pieces of butter, and bake in hot oven for twenty minutes. When cooked sprinkle with the juice of a lemon and serve in the baking dish.

**Broiled Smelts.** — Split and clean as many smelts as are required. Select large ones. Remove the backbone, rub each one with olive oil, and season with a little salt and pepper. Grease the broiler, arrange the smelts on it, and broil on each side for two or three minutes. Serve with a Béarnaise sauce.

**Smelt Croquettes.** — Select as many medium-sized fresh smelts as you desire to serve. Clean and prepare them as you would for broiling, removing backbone, dry them, and set in cool place. Boil one pound of halibut, pound it fine, then add a little Sherry, white pepper and salt to taste. Beat in enough cream sauce to enable you to form the mixture into small croquettes. Roll a smelt around each one, fastening it by sticking the head through the tail. Roll in beaten egg and fine bread crumbs and fry in hot lard. Drain on thick brown paper. Arrange a lemon basket in the centre of a dish, around it place the smelts and garnish border with half of the whites of hard-boiled eggs, each filled with tartare sauce.

**Fried Smelts à la Parisienne.** — Wash the smelts thoroughly, cut down the back, and take the bone out a little below the head and just above the tail. Clean well and cut away the fins and gills. Dry well and flour them. Roll them up by putting their tails in their mouths and fastening them with a little wooden skewer. Set away in the ice-box. Have your oil or fat very hot. Fry a few at a time, then let your oil get very hot. Put all in your frying basket, plunge into your hot fat. They will swell up and be a beautiful brown and crisp. Boil the number of eggs required, allowing one-half for each person. Take out the yolks and put the whites in cold water. Make a tartare sauce. When ready to serve, fill each half egg with tartare sauce and put round the fish. Put a bunch of parsley between each egg. Serve the fish very hot.

**Sauted Smelts.** — Clean and wipe nine selected smelts. Cut five parallel gashes on both sides of each fish. Sprinkle with salt, pepper, and lemon juice ; cover and let stand fifteen minutes. Dip in cream, dredge with flour, and sauté in butter until delicately browned, taking care that butter in pan does not burn. Pour around smelts a sauce made from butter in pan : one tablespoonful flour, and one cup of chicken stock, and seasoned with salt, pepper, and lemon juice.

**Stuffed Smelts.** — Remove the fins from two dozen large smelts. Clean them without splitting them and stuff with a fish forcemeat — a paper cornucopia must be used. Place the fish on a well-buttered dish, cover them with one pint of Italienne sauce, and bake in a hot oven for ten minutes. Squeeze some lemon juice over them and serve in the same dish.

**Baked Sardines, No. 1.** — Remove the skin from twelve large sardines. Put them on a dish and heat them through. Put the oil from the sardines in a saucepan, and when it comes to a boil stir in one cup of water, then add one teaspoonful of Worcestershire sauce, salt and pepper to taste. Remove from the fire, and stir in the beaten yolk of an egg, one teaspoonful of vinegar, and one of mustard. Serve the fish very hot, with this sauce poured over them or in a separate dish.

**Baked Sardines, No. 2.** — To one small can of sardines allow two tablespoonfuls of butter, four tablespoonfuls of bread crumbs and one small onion, finely minced, and two eggs, salt and pepper to taste ; wipe all the oil from the sardines, divide them into halves and lay in a baking dish ; melt half the butter, pour it over them and add two tablespoonfuls of hot water ; beat up the eggs and gradually mix them into the bread crumbs, onion, salt and pepper and remainder of the butter; spread this mixture over the sardines and bake fifteen minutes.

**Sardines au Gratin.** — Heat a tablespoonful of oil in an earthen baking dish, add one exceedingly fine chopped onion and gently brown five minutes, frequently stirring meanwhile, Wipe neatly and split open through front twelve good-sized sardines in oil, bone them, arrange them in dish over the onions. Knead in a bowl one ounce fresh butter, one-half teaspoonful fresh chopped parsley, two tablespoonfuls fresh bread crumbs and one-half a bean finely chopped garlic. Divide mixture in small bits over sardines, set in a very brisk oven for six minutes, remove and immediately send to the table in same dish.

**Sardine Salad.** — Cover a large plate with lettuce leaves, letting them come over the edge of the dish. Take any kind of boiled white fish that has been " left over " and pick into small pieces, covering the lettuce, leaving a narrow margin; split six sardines, taking out the bone and lay them on the fish, the heads in the centre, and spread around to form a disk; put a little parsley in the middle of the dish, at the heads and on the fish, between each sardine put a generous teaspoonful of mayonnaise, slice a lemon and cut each slice in half and garnish the edge of the fish, the rind lying on lettuce.

**Sardine Sandwiches.** — Take as many boneless sardines as are required, open each one lengthwise, being careful not to break them, and place the halves on a fine wire broiler. When they have broiled a little on each side, set them away to cool. When cold, squeeze a little lemon juice over them, and cut off the tails. If fresh butter is used on the bread, sprinkle a little salt over the sardines while they are hot. Allow two halves to a triangle of bread, and make according to directions. Ordinary canned sardines may be used without broiling, but they are apt to be very oily.

**Fillet of Sole, No. 1.** — Cut off the head and tail of a large flounder and set away for future use. Cut off the fillets from the fish and bake them in the oven for ten minutes and set them away to cool. Then make a puree of mushrooms in the following way: Peel and chop fine one pound of mushrooms, melt one ounce of butter, add one ounce of flour, and let them come to a boil. Then stir in one-half cup of consomme, half a cup of cream, and the mushrooms and boil for five minutes. Then set the mixture away to cool. Make a forcemeat of halibut or any kind of fish desired. Now lay the fish fillets on a platter, cover each one with the mushroom puree, and then with the forcemeat. Put the head and tail in place. Set the platter in a pan of hot water and bake in a moderate oven for ten minutes. Remove carefully to a platter, garnish with parsley, and serve with Hollandaise sauce.

**Fillet of Sole, No. 2.** — Take two soles, divide them from the backbone, remove the heads, fins, and tails. Sprinkle the inside with pepper, salt, and the juice of half a lemon. Roll in the shape of a corkscrew, then roll them in egg, then fresh bread crumbs, then in egg, and bread crumbs again. Fry in hot fat and serve on a napkin. Garnish with lemon baskets filled with tartare sauce and sprigs of parsley.

**Chartreuse of Fish a la Hauraise.** — Take some nice fillets of sole, put them on a buttered baking tin. Season them with salt, pepper, and a little lemon juice. Cover them with a thick buttered paper and cook them in a moderate oven for six or eight minutes. Then take up the fillets and put them to press until cold. Cut them out with a plain round cutter, ornament half of them with coral (lobster's), and the other half with tarragon and parsley and truffle. Set the garnish with a little liquid aspic jelly. Line the chartreuse mold with aspic jelly and arrange the rounds of sole all over the mold. Set this with aspic, just enough to make the garnish firm, and in the centre place the following mixture :

Take about half a pint of picked shrimps or lobsters, cut in dice shapes, two peeled tomatoes, four artichoke bottoms (cooked and cold), and twelve raw oysters. Add seasoning and red pepper and trimmings of sole. Mix all with half pint of liquid aspic jelly and two large tablespoonfuls of thick mayonnaise sauce. Stir all together on ice till it begins to set, then pour into the mold as directed. Let it stand an hour or more, turn out on stand, and garnish with jelly.

**Sole Normande, with Sauce.** — Butter a tin very quickly. Boil some onions in water to remove the strong flavor, then slice them very thin and lay them on the butter. Place the sole on them. Put over it salt, pepper, and nutmeg to taste, also some chopped parsley. Add the juice of one lemon and as much white wine as will cover it. Place them in a slow oven for thirty minutes. Baste the sole with its own liquor very often, and add more butter if required. Serve with fried bread sippets and a sauce made from the gravy in which the fish has been cooked.

### Sandwiches of Fillets of Sole, Lobster, or Salmon. —

Cook the fillets of sole in a saucepan with a little clarified butter, pepper, salt, and lemon juice. When done, put them in press between two dishes. When cold, divide each fillet into four pieces, trim, and put in a bowl with a French dressing made of white pepper, salt, vinegar, and oil. Have some small oval rolls at hand, cut off the tops and remove the crumbs, moisten the bottom of each roll with a littte of the dressing, place a piece of sole on this, add a little mayonnaise sauce, cover with the tops, and serve. Sandwiches of lobster and salmon are prepared in the same manner. If desired, each one may have a finely chopped onion sprinkled over it before the mayonnaise is added.

### Fillets of Sole a la Venitienne. —

Take the fillets of four soles, trim and place one-half of them in a saucepan with some clarified butter, a little lemon juice, white pepper, and salt. Let them simmer slowly for ten minutes. Simmer the other fillets, without trimming them, in the same manner. When they are done, drain them and set away to cool. Cut the untrimmed fillets into small dice. Mix them with some thick Allemande sauce, two ounces of grated Parmesan cheese, white pepper and salt to taste, and a dash of grated nutmeg. Spread this preparation about one-sixth of an inch thick on an earthen dish, and when it has become firm cut it into pieces about the size and shape of the fillets. Roll them in fine bread crumbs, then in beaten egg, and then again in bread crumbs. Just before serving warm the fillets, fry the croquettes in hot lard, drain both on a piece of brown paper. Arrange them in a close circle, placing alternately the croquettes and the fillets. Fill the centre with small fish forcemeat balls, fried in hot lard. Pour some Venitienne sauce in the centre and on the fillets and serve.

### Fish Timbales. —

Take a cup of any cold cooked fish; pick it over carefully, season with salt and pepper, add a tablespoonful of chopped parsley and enough white sauce to make hold together.  Butter mold, turn the fish in, stand it in a pan of hot water, bake in oven for one-half hour.

**Tongues and Sounds.** — Soak the tongues and sounds in cold water over night.  Put them in cold water and place on the fire.  Let them boil thirty minutes and serve with drawn butter.

**Turbot à la Crême.** — In place of turbot, either bass or codfish will answer.  Boil with plenty of salt, remove the skin and bones, and flake it.  Boil one quart of cream, and while boiling stir in three tablespoonfuls of flour, perfectly smooth, and add a bunch of parsley and one onion.  Take out both vegetables.  Clarify a quarter of a pound of butter and add to the cream after it is boiled.  Butter a deep dish, and put in first a layer of fish, then one of sauce, alternating till the dish is filled, making the sauce come on top.  Strew over a layer of sifted bread crumbs and bake an hour.  Garnish the dish with chopped eggs or parsley.

# FISH AND MEAT SAUCES.

Many people fail in making sauces by not cooking the flour sufficiently, and also by serving them with a mass of oily butter on the surface. Usually the flour is wet to a smooth paste and stirred into the boiling liquid. When made in this manner, the sauce should boil at least ten minutes to have the flour thoroughly cooked. But by cooking the dry flour in the hot butter the starch in the flour is more quickly cooked, and the butter is all absorbed and converted into an emulsion. Sauces made in this manner are perfectly smooth, free from grease, and have a fine flavor. Every one should learn how to make both white and brown sauces. They are adapted to nearly every form of food. Meats, fish, vegetables, eggs, macaroni, rice, toast, etc., are rendered more palatable by being served with an appropriate sauce.

**How to Make Sauce.** — Melt a tablespoonful of butter in saucepan and add a tablespoonful of flour. Strain the gravy from the pan in which the fish has been cooked. Add a full cup of it to the butter and flour. Let it come to a boil, then cook five minutes. Season to taste, add one-half cup of rich cream. Serve very hot in sauce-boat.

**Brown Sauce.** — One pint hot stock, two tablespoonfuls minced onion, two tablespoonfuls butter, two heaping tablespoonfuls flour, one-half teaspoonful salt, one-half saltspoonful pepper, one tablespoonful lemon juice, caramel enough to color.

Mince the onion and fry it in the butter five minutes. Be careful not to burn it. When the butter is brown, add the dry flour and stir well. Add the hot stock a little at a time and stir rapidly, as it thickens, until perfectly smooth. Add the salt and pepper, using more if high seasoning is desired. Simmer five minutes, and strain to remove the onion.

The stock for brown sauces may be made from bones and remnants of any kind of meat, by soaking them in cold water, and boiling until the nutriment is extracted. The onion may be omitted if the flavor be not desired; but the sauce is better with it if it be not burned.

By the addition of different seasoning materials to this brown sauce a great variety of sauces may be made. Half the quantity given is sufficient for most entrees, or to use for any purpose in a small family.   Be careful not to burn the butter, as the desired color can better be obtained by adding caramel.

**Drawn Butter, No. 1.** — To one heaping tablespoonful of butter take one heaping tablespoonful of flour, a little salt, and enough hot water to dissolve this cream.   Thicken by standing the saucepan in hot water.   Chopped parsley or the crushed yolks of hard-boiled eggs may be added to this.   Let it stand (covered) in the hot water until ready to serve.

**Drawn Butter, No. 2.** — One-half cup butter, two table-spoonfuls flour; rub thoroughly together, then stir into pint boiling water; little salt; parsley if wished.

**Tomato Sauce, No. 1.** — Simmer one-half can tomatoes, one chopped onion, one-half teaspoonful salt, one-fourth tea-spoonful pepper, one clove together ten minutes.   Rub through sieve.   Cook together one tablespoonful each of flour and butter one minute, add tomato gradually, stir till smooth, and simmer five minutes.

**Hollandaise Sauce.** — Cream one-half cup butter; add gradually two beaten egg yolks; stir well.   Add one tablespoonful lemon juice, dash each of salt and cayenne.   Add one-half cup boiling water, and stir over boiling water till thick as boiled custard.   Serve immediately.

**Sauce Tartare, No. 1.** — Make one cup mayonnaise.   Chop very fine one tablespoonful each of capers, olives, green cucumber pickle, and parsley.   Press in a cloth till quite dry.   Blend gradually with the mayonnaise.   For fried or broiled fish.

**Maître d'Hôtel Butter, No. 1.** — Cream two tablespoonfuls butter, add gradually one-half teaspoonful salt, one-eighth tea-spoonful white pepper, one tablespoonful each of lemon juice and chopped parsley.   Keep very cold.   Serve with fried fish or broiled steak.

**Horse-radish Sauce.** — Cream two tablespoonfuls butter; add two tablespoonfuls fresh grated horse-radish, one tablespoon-ful very thick cream, one-half teaspoonful lemon juice.   Keep very cold.   Good with corned beef.

**Mint Sauce.** — One cup chopped green mint leaves, one-half cup vinegar, one-fourth cup powdered sugar. Mix one hour before serving with lamb.

**Mayonnaise Salad Dressing.** — Have dishes and ingredients very cold. If summer, set dish in pan of pounded ice. In soup-plate or shallow bowl put yolk one raw egg, add one-fourth teaspoonful salt and dash cayenne, a few drops of tabasco and a teaspoonful Worcestershire sauce, stir with fork till very thick. Add few drops olive oil and stir; add more oil, few drops at a time, until mixture balls on fork. Thin with few drops lemon juice or vinegar, then add more oil. Alternate in this way until one cup olive oil is used and dressing is thick and glossy, like a jelly. About three tablespoonfuls lemon juice or two of vinegar will be needed, according to its acidity. *Always stir in the same direction.* Keep covered and on ice until needed.

**Clam Sauce.** — Take one quart of freshly opened Little Neck clams, half pint of water, an ounce of butter, and boil five minutes. Mix two ounces of butter, one ounce of flour, and a little nutmeg together, and add one-half pint of boiling water, and one-half pint of clam liquor. Stir with egg-beater, boil a minute or two, add two egg yolks, twice as much water as egg yolks, and a little lemon juice. Strain through a wet cloth. Then mix in four ounces of butter, drain the clams, put them in the sauce, and serve hot.

**Court Bouillon for all Sorts of Fresh Water Fish.** — One pint of water, one quart of white wine, one tablespoonful of butter, a bunch of parsley, a few young onions, one clove of garlic, a bunch of thyme, one bay leaf, one carrot, and a blade of mace. Boil the fish in this bouillon, which will do for use several times. Any kind of fish, such as salmon, trout, pompano, sheepshead, carp, may be boiled in this way. Lobster boiled in court bouillon is very fine.

**Egg Sauce, No. 1.** — Mix together three ounces of butter, two ounces of flour, a little nutmeg, and salt and pepper. Do not melt the butter. Add one pint of boiling water, and stir with whip to get sauce smooth. Then boil for a moment. Stir in the yolks of two eggs, four ounces butter, and a little lemon juice. Press through a wet cloth and add two hard-boiled eggs, chopped fine.

**Herb Sauce.** — Place two chopped shallots in a saucepan with a little butter, salt, white pepper, grated nutmeg, and a glass of white wine. Boil until it is reduced one-half. Add half a pint of veloute sauce and boil a minute. Thicken with three egg yolks and as much water as you have egg yolks, mix water and yolks together, and stir without boiling. Then add carefully four ounces of butter in small bits, stirring all the while. Finish with chopped parsley and lemon juice.

**Lobster Sauce.** — After removing the meat from a good-sized boiled lobster, boil the shells in one scant quart of water for twenty minutes. Strain and use the broth to make a cream sauce. Cut the lobster meat in small pieces and powder the dried lobster coral. Stir both into the sauce. Add a dash of cayenne and two tablespoonfuls of lemon juice.

**Martinot Sauce for Fish.** — Cook one tablespoonful of butter, one tablespoonful of flour, one teaspoonful of chopped onion, one-half can of tomatoes, one-half teaspoonful of sugar, one-half teaspoonful of salt, all together for ten minutes. Strain into another saucepan and add the yolks of four eggs with one tablespoonful of cream and a little nutmeg. Set the pan in hot water and add four ounces of butter, *small piece at a time.* Set over the fire and stir until smooth. Then remove trom fire and add a little lemon juice or tarragon vinegar. Strain through a strainer and then add a little whipped cream.

**Mussel Sauce.** — Cleanse, wash, and blanch or stew two quarts of mussels. Remove the meat from the shells and place where it will keep warm. Reserve the liquor in a basin. Knead four ounces of butter with two ounces of flour, add some white pepper, a dash of grated nutmeg, and salt. Stir in the liquor from the mussels and half a pint of cream. Then add a mixture of four egg yolks and twice as much water as you have egg liquid. Stir over the fire until the sauce becomes the desired consistency. Strain through a wet cloth and pour over the mussels. Just before sending to the table add some finely chopped parsley and a little lemon juice.

**Shad Sauce.** — Four shallots, chopped very fine. Put them in a saucepan with two ounces butter and four tablespoonfuls of white wine vinegar. Let it boil down to half the original quantity, then add one pint veloute sauce. Boil a little longer, add finely chopped parsley, tarragon, and about four ounces of butter in small bits. Mix thoroughly.

**Shrimp Sauce.** — Beat a scant cup of butter to a cream, then stir in two tablespoonfuls of flour. Beat until light, then pour in one and a half tablespoonfuls of anchovy and one tablespoonful of lemon juice. Mix this with a pint of boiling water. Mix thoroughtly and stir over the fire until it is just about to boil. Stir in two gills of fresh shrimp with the tails split and add a dash of cayenne. Let the sauce get very hot and serve at once.

**Tomato Sauce, No. 2.** — One-fourth of a can of tomatoes, one white onion cut up and fried a little in two tablespoonfuls of butter, one-half teaspoonful of beef extract which has been diluted in a little water, four cloves of garlic, salt and pepper to taste, and finally one teaspoonful of corn-starch, dissolved in water.

**Tartare Sauce** for Fried Clams, Scallops and all kinds of Fish. — Mix some finely chopped pickles or olives or a mixture of both with salad cream. Another combination preferred by some is finely chopped pickles, capers and parsley.

**Tartare Sauce, No. 2.** — Season Mayonnaise dressing to taste with finely chopped shallots, capers, and vinegar pickles. If too thick, thin it with vinegar.

**Maître d'Hôtel Butter, No. 2.** — Cream one-quarter cup of butter. Add one-half teaspoonful salt, a dash of pepper and a tablespoonful of fine chopped parsley ; then, very slowly, to avoid curdling, a tablespoonful of lemon juice. This sauce is appropriate also for beefsteak and broiled fish.

**Fish Cream.** — Run cold cooked fish through the chopper to the amount of two cupfuls. Pour one cupful of boiling water over one cupful of fine bread crumbs. Let this mixture stand fifteen minutes, then add the fish, a half teaspoonful of salt, a pinch of white pepper, a tablespoonful of minced olives or parsley, two tablespoonfuls of melted butter and two well-beaten eggs. Pour into a well-buttered mold, steam in a steamer for three-quarters of an hour. Serve as soon as unmolded on a hot platter, served with tomato sauce. This makes a very nice dish for a luncheon.

# OYSTERS.

Oysters, Clams, Scallops, Lobsters, Crabs, Shrimps, and Prawns are the principal varieties of shell fish used as food.

These shell fish are found in perfection in the cool waters of the Northern Atlantic coast. The Wareham and the Providence River are esteemed in Boston. Oysters are neither healthful nor well flavored from May to September; at all other times they are used more extensively and are more highly prized than any other shell fish. They are nutritious, are easily digested when fresh and eaten raw, or when only slightly cooked. When over-cooked, they are tough and leathery. Oysters should never be kept long after being taken from the shell; and if to be used raw should not be opened till just before using.

**To Prepare Oysters for Cooking.** — Pour half a cup of cold water over one quart of oysters; take out each oyster separately with fingers and free from any bits of shell. The oyster liquor may be strained and used in soup, stew, or escallop if desired. Fried and broiled oysters are much better and cook easier if parboiled slightly before crumbing. Place one pint of cleaned oysters in a frying basket and keep it for one-half minute in a kettle of boiling water deep enough to cover them. Drain, dry on a soft towel and proceed as usual.

**Oysters a la Bechamel.** — Drain one pint oysters and save the liquor; for twenty-five oysters add milk to the liquor to make half a pint. Put one tablespoonful butter and one of flour in chafing-dish, then light the lamp; mix thoroughly; add liquor and milk, stir until it reaches the boiling point; add oysters, half a teaspoonful salt, a quarter teaspoonful black pepper, and a dash of red pepper; cover the dish, and when boiling, stir in lastly the yolks of three eggs beaten with two tablespoonfuls of cream; after putting out the light add a teaspoonful of lemon juice, half a teaspoonful of onion juice, and serve on toast.

**Oysters a la Beleveu.** — One-quarter pound butter melted in chafing-dish; add one-half cup finely chopped celery and cook thoroughly; put in one quart cream (or milk) with juice of oysters; allow it to just come to a boil, then add one pint of oysters; add a dash of paprika, salt and pepper, and just before serving add a wine-glass Madeira wine.

**Oyster Bisque.** — Two quarts of oysters in a saucepan with a little white pepper, nutmeg, two blades of mace, one bay leaf, one pinch of red pepper, two ounces of butter, one pint of white broth. Cover, boil ten minutes, drain in a colander, and save the liquor. Then chop the oysters very fine and put them on a plate. Knead five ounces of flour in a saucepan with four ounces of melted butter. Stir and cook a little without allowing to brown. Then dilute with three pints of boiled milk and the oyster liquor. Add the oysters, stir steadily, and boil ten minutes. Rub through a very fine sieve and add more milk if required. Stir and boil again. Finish with one-half pint of raw cream and four ounces of butter in small bits. Taste, pour in soup tureen, and serve hot, with small squares of bread fried in butter separately on a plate.

**Baked in Shells, No. 1.** — Take large oysters, dry between towels, dip in egg, then in dry bread crumbs that have been seasoned with salt, pepper, and a grating of nutmeg. Put the oysters in their shells, dot with butter, lay the shells in a dripping pan and bake till brown. Serve at once in their shells, with a dash of lemon juice on each.

**Baked Oysters, No. 2.** — Put a round of toasted bread into a small baking cup or dish; spread with butter and fill with oysters; season with salt, pepper, and butter. Fill as many cups as required, place them in a baking pan in oven, cover with a pan and bake about ten minutes.

**Broiled Oysters, No. 1.** — Take the largest oysters, scald, drain, dry on a towel and dip one by one into softened butter till well coated and then in seasoned flour. Lay them on a buttered broiler. Cook over clear coals until a light brown. Serve on slices of buttered thin toast. If done by a gas stove, lay the toast under the broiler to catch the drip. Fine cracker crumbs may be used instead of flour. Oysters that have been breaded for frying are good broiled.

**Broiled Oysters, No. 2.** — Take two dozen large oysters, cleaned, drained, and dried in a soft cloth. Sprinkle with salt and pepper. Melt two ounces butter in a large frying-pan, lay in one dozen; as soon as the last one is in, turn the first one and when all have been turned, begin taking out, laying them closely on a large buttered oyster broiler; cook to a light brown over

moderate fire. While these are browning, the other dozen may
" set " in the butter. Have six rounds of toast on a hot platter;
put four oysters on each, sprinkle on the butter in which they
were stiffened and serve with lemon cut in eighths.

**Broiled Oysters, No. 3.** — Look over the oysters, rejecting
bits of shells; dry between towels; dip in melted butter or olive
oil seasoned with salt and pepper; heat the oyster broiler, wipe
over with butter; lay on the oysters and broil over a clear fire —
charcoal is best — for four or five minutes, turning often; serve
on rounds of toasted bread, spread with butter and slightly
moistened with the oyster liquor (which has been heated), garnish
with sprigs of parsley and lemon. These are delicious served
with pickled peaches.

**Broiled Oysters, No. 4.** — Pick, wash, and drain large
oysters. Dip each in melted butter, roll in fine crumbs, and
broil in fine wire broiler over a clear, hot fire. Serve on toast
with sliced lemons.

**Broiled Oysters, No. 5.** — Drain on a towel as many large
oysters as are required. Dip them in melted butter, then in
cracker crumbs which have been seasoned with pepper and salt.
Lay them on a well-buttered fine broiler and broil until slightly
colored.

**Broiled Oysters, No. 6.** — Drain select oysters in a colander. Dip them one by one into melted butter, to prevent sticking to the gridiron, and place them on a wire gridiron. Broil
over a clear fire. When nicely browned on both sides, season
with salt, pepper, and plenty of butter, and lay them on hot
buttered toast, moistened with a little hot water. Serve very
hot. Oysters cooked in this way and served on broiled beefsteak
are delicious.

**Creamed Oysters, No. 1.** — Prepare cream sauce, taking
one-half the quantity of butter; scald the oysters until the edges
begin to curl, drain and drop them into the cream sauce; let all
stand in bain marie for five minutes to season thoroughly. Serve
in Swedish timbales or in pate shells. It is very nice used as a
filling for short cake, croustade, or on toast.

**Creamed Oysters, No. 2.** — Fifty shell oysters, one quart sweet cream; butter, pepper, and salt to suit taste. Put the cream and oysters in separate kettles to heat, the oysters in their own liquor, and let them come to a boil; when sufficiently cooked, skim; then take them out of the liquid and put them into a dish to keep warm. Put the cream and liquid together. Season to taste, and thicken with powdered cracker. When sufficiently thick, stir in the oysters.

**Creamed Oysters, No. 3.** — Melt four tablespoonfuls butter in chafing-dish; then add five tablespoonfuls flour, mixed with one-quarter teaspoonful salt and one-eighth teaspoonful pepper; pour on gradually one pint milk and stir; when sauce thickens, add one pint oysters without liquor; cook until edges curl; serve on buttered toast.

**Creamed Oysters, No. 4.** — Prepare one cup thick cream sauce (see Sauces). Pan one pint cleaned oysters; drain and add to sauce. Season with salt, pepper, pinch of mace, and a few drops lemon juice.

**Creamed Oysters for Croustades.** — Cook for two minutes one ounce of flour and one ounce of butter. Stir in one-half cup of milk and two tablespoonfuls of mushroom liquor. Let the mixture come to a boil, then add one-half cup of cream, one-half tablespoonful of salt, a dash of cayenne, and a little nutmeg. Wash one quart of medium-sized oysters, cutting out the hard part. Stir them into the sauce. Let them come to a boil or until they begin to curl. Fill each croustade with the mixture and serve very hot.

**Oyster Croustades.** — Take six nice pieces of butter the size of an egg. Shape them a little wider at one end than the other. Roll them thickly in bread crumbs, then in beaten yolks of three eggs, then again in bread crumbs. Set them on ice for half an hour. When cold, drop them, one by one, in boiling fat and fry until a delicate brown. With a sharp knife take off the tops. Let the butter run out, and fill each one with creamed oysters. Garnish with parsley and serve them very hot.

**Oyster Cocktail, No. 1.** — Place six very small and thoroughly chilled oysters in a glass that will hold as much as a claret glass. To each glass add two drops of tabasco sauce, one teaspoonful of Worcestershire sauce, one dessertspoonful of catsup, and a little lemon juice or vinegar. Serve very cold.

**Oyster Cocktail, No. 2.** — Serve in small glasses, five small oysters to a glass. Cover with tomato catsup, add one drop of tabasco sauce to each glass, also a little horse-radish and a few drops of lemon juice. Prepare mixture and let oysters stand in it for at least three hours before serving.

**Cromeskies.** — Have at hand thirty-five oysters, an equal quantity of cooked chicken, three or four mushrooms, two teaspoonfuls of cream, three eggs, some frying batter, some slices of very thin and fat bacon, and some parsley. Scald the oysters in their own liquor. Remove the hard part, also the black edge or beard, as it is called. Cut the part remaining into small pieces, also the chicken and mushrooms very fine. Make a cream sauce, add the liquor the oysters were scalded in, and boil until it is very thick. A little cream, if you have it, could be added. Mix it with the oysters, chicken, and mushrooms; stir in the yolks of three eggs, stir it over the fire for three or four minutes. Spread the mixture on a dish and set it away to cool. When thoroughly cold, roll into pieces about the size and shape of a good-sized cork, wrap each one in a very thin slice of bacon. Dip each one in batter and fry in hot lard. When a nice brown, drain on brown paper and serve on hot plate with a garnish of fried parsley.

**Oyster Croquettes, No. 1.** — Cook slightly one quart of oysters in their own liquor. Make a sauce as follows : Heat two tablespoonfuls of butter, stir in two tablespoonfuls of flour, then stir in one-half cup of cream and some of the oyster liquor. Cook until the mixture is a thick sauce. Season with a few drops of Sherry, salt, white pepper, and a dash of cayenne. Chop the oysters very fine and add to the sauce. Set away to cool. When cold, shape into croquettes, roll in beaten egg, then in fine bread crumbs, and fry in hot fat. Drain on heavy brown paper. Serve with cream sauce in a separate dish.

**Oyster Croquettes, No. 2.** — Boil two quarts of oysters, with a little broth, pepper, very little ground mace, and two ounces of butter, for two minutes. Then drain on a sieve. Cool them a little and save the liquor. Then slice the oysters; *do not chop them*. Mix two ounces of butter, one ounce of flour, and one tablespoonful of chopped shallots. Cook them until slightly browned, then add one-half pint of the oyster liquor. Stir and boil five minutes. Then add the beaten yolks of four eggs, the sliced oysters, a little chopped parsley, and a dash of red pepper. Stir constantly and boil three minutes longer. Then stir in the juice of one lemon and set away to cool. When cold, divide the mixture into pieces the size of an egg, roll them in pulverized crackers, and with the blade of a knife give them a rectangular shape about one inch thick. Dip in beaten eggs, then in crackers again, and fry a light brown in plenty of clear hot lard. Dish up on a folded napkin, garnish with fried parsley and quartered lemons, and serve.

**Masked Oyster Cutlets.** — Pick fresh crab or lobster meat very fine and mix with enough mashed and seasoned potato to make a paste. Have the oysters drained and dried on a cloth, seasoned with pepper and salt, then remove the muscular part of the oyster, lay two together and cover with the potato mixture. Dip in beaten egg and then in crumbs mixed with a little crab meat, and fry a dainty brown. Serve with sauce tartare or Bearnaise sauce.

**Oysters en Casserole.** — Butter individual casseroles and sprinkle the bottom of each with finely minced or chopped green pepper, onion, parsley and pinch of clove. Brown the onion and pepper a little. Add a thin small strip of bacon that has been fried crisp ; then season the oysters. Sprinkle a very little of the onion, parsley, and green pepper over the top and criss-cross with two tiny bacon strips. Put on the covers and bake just long enough to heat thoroughly, then uncover and brown the bacon quickly. Replace the covers and serve at once with cut lemon.

**Curried Oysters.** — Cook one quart of oysters over a slow fire in their own juice. If the juice is not sufficient to cook them add a little water. Add also a tablespoonful of butter, a teaspoonful of curry powder, and salt and pepper to taste. When the oysters are firm, stir in one tablespoonful of flour moistened to a paste with water. Stir carefully and thoroughly while the liquor thickens.

**Deviled Oysters.** — One heaping saltspoonful dry mustard, one-half saltspoonful each pepper and salt and the yolk of one egg. Mix to a smooth paste and coat six large oysters with it.

Roll them in fine crumbs and broil over a clear fire. Arrange and serve.

**Fried Oysters, No. 1.**—Select large oysters, clean, and parboil slightly to draw out some of the water. Drain and dry on a towel. Roll in fine bread and cracker crumbs, dip in mayonnaise dressing, then in crumbs again. Let them stand five minutes, and if they seem moist, dip again in crumbs, and cook in deep hot fat for one minute. Being already cooked, they only need to be thoroughly heated and the crumbs browned.

**Fried Oysters, No. 2.**—Pick over, scald and drain dry two dozen oysters, sprinkle lightly with red pepper, roll in cracker dust, dip in egg mixed with an equal quantity of thick cream ; drain and roll in fresh fine bread crumbs ; press gently with a palette knife, fry half a dozen at a time in clear fat, hot enough to brown them in one minute. As soon as the first basket is lifted, drop in a half a dozen slices of raw potato to keep the fat from burning while the oysters are changed for another half dozen ; proceed in this way until all are done. Put in a whole potato in slices and take from the fire at once ; with a little care the same fat may be used repeatedly, when otherwise it would be blackened the first time. Drain the oysters on soft brown paper. Have a tuft of parsley on a hot folded napkin ; range the oysters quickly and serve instantly. It is better not to begin frying until they are wanted than to delay serving. Nothing can be less inviting than a cold fried oyster or one that has been kept hot for five minutes.

*Philadelphia Fry :* Proceed as before, but after they are rolled in crumbs the first time, dip them in very cold, thick mayonnaise, then into egg, and roll in crumbs again before frying. This is difficult but delicious.

*Sauteed :* To one pint prepared oysters put one pint stale bread crumbs, season and add two eggs beaten lightly. Let them stand one hour, then lay by spoonfuls in a frying-pan and brown quickly on both sides in hot butter. Serve at once.

**Fried Oysters, No. 3.**—Select the largest and finest fresh oysters, put them into a colander and pour over a little water to rinse them ; then place them on a clean towel and dry them. Have ready some grated bread crumbs seasoned with pepper and salt, and plenty of yolk of egg beaten till very light ; and to each egg allow a large teaspoonful of rich cream or of the best fresh butter. Beat the egg and cream together. Dip each oyster first into the egg and cream and then into the crumbs. Repeat this twice, until the oysters are well coated all over. Have ready boiling, in a frying-pan, an equal mixture of fresh butter and lard. It must very nearly fill the frying-pan, and be boiling fast when the oysters go in, otherwise they will be heavy and greasy. Fry them a yellow brown on both sides and serve hot.

**Fried Oysters, No. 4.** — Select the largest oysters, drain and dry between towels ; dip in beaten egg, then in dry sifted bread crumbs which have been seasoned with salt and pepper, and fry in a wire basket in deep fat.

These may be prepared some hours before cooking and the breading process repeated after the first coat is dry.

**Fried Oysters, No. 5.** — Select largest and finest oysters. Drain and wipe them by spreading upon cloth, laying another over them, pressing lightly. Roll each in beaten egg, then in cracker crumbs with which has been mixed a very little pepper. Fry in mixture of equal parts of lard and butter.

**Oysters Fried in Batter.** — One cup of milk, two eggs well beaten, pepper, salt, and flour to make a moderately stiff batter.

Add one cup of oysters with their liquor, season with grated nutmeg, and drop by spoonfuls into deep fat and fry. One-half a teaspoonful of baking powder sifted into the flour will make a light and puffy batter. If preferred the oysters may be dipped in the batter one at a time, but small oysters are better when mixed with the batter.

**Fricassee of Oysters, No. 1.** — Select thirty medium-sized oysters. Place them in their own liquor on the stove and let come to a boil. Skim them and pour in a strainer. Heat one tablespoonful of butter, add two tablespoonfuls of flour, mix thoroughly and then stir in the oyster liquor and half a pint of cream. Season with white pepper, a dash of cayenne, and salt. Beat thoroughly the yolks of two eggs with the juice of half a lemon. Stir into the sauce. Then add the oysters and serve very hot.

**Oyster Fricassee, No. 2.** — Melt one cup of butter in the frying-pan, add one quart of oysters, let come to a boil, then add one-half cup of cream with salt and pepper to taste and one tablespoonful of flour mixed with a little cold milk; cook till the oysters are done; remove from the fire and add the yolks of two well-beaten eggs, pour over a platter of hot toasted crackers.

**White Fricassee of Oysters.** — Put one tablespoonful of butter into a frying-pan and when hot put in one pint of oysters washed and drained. Cook till plump and drain again. Pour the oyster liquor into a cup and fill with cream. Cook one table-spoonful flour with one of butter and blend with cream and oyster liquor; add one-half saltspoonful pepper and about one-half teaspoonful salt. (Oysters vary in freshness.) Beat one egg very light and pour the oyster sauce upon it; add the oysters and return to the pan to be well heated, but it must not boil. Stir gently that it may cook evenly. Serve in crust or pastry shells if for lunch or dinner; for breakfast or tea on toast.

**Brown Fricassee of Oysters.** — One quart oysters, two large tablespoonfuls butter, one scant tablespoonful flour, a dust of cayenne, salt according to the oysters, and one-half teaspoon-ful chopped parsley. Brown the butter and flour, add the oysters prepared as directed, stir carefully not to break them, and as soon as they curl serve on a hot platter with eight triangles of toast, one for each portion.

**Griddled Oysters.** — Clean, scald, and drain two dozen large oysters. Have a large griddle evenly heated; drop on it a bit of sweet butter as large as a pea and put an oyster on it; lay on one dozen and give them plenty of room; put on another bit of butter and turn the first oyster on to that; proceed in this way for all. Do not let them burn, but they must brown quickly. If too much butter is put on it will spread over the griddle and scorch and the smoke will ruin the oysters. Serve four to each person on a two-inch square of rye shortcake.

**Hunter's Cake.** — Chop some ·fresh button mushrooms, chives, parsley and shallots together, and sprinkle over the oysters after they are drained and placed in buttered oblong baking dishes of individual size, covered with buttered crumbs, and bake in a quick oven until crumbs brown, from five to eight minutes. Serve with sliced lemon or maître d'hôtel butter.

**Oysters a la Lincoln.** — Line as many cases — metal, paper, or china — as desired with veal forcemeat for fish. Poach one quart of medium-sized oysters in their own liquor with one gill of white wine. When cooked, drain and pare them. Cut them in half-inch-sized pieces and fill each case with these. Chop some raw mushrooms and fry them for a few minutes in a little butter and place them on top of the oysters. Cover with veloute sauce, which has been mixed with the oyster liquor and then boiled down. Cover then with another layer of forcemeat. Brush each one with melted butter. Bake on tin sheet in a slack oven for fifteen minutes.

**Oysters a la Louise** (*Chafing-dish*). — Cook in melted butter some cepes, cut up small, then add twelve oysters, one small piece of lobster coral, then stir in one-quarter of a pound of cream and the yokes of two fresh eggs. Just before serving add one small glass of Sherry. — *Waldorf Astoria.*

**Oyster Loaf.** — Cut a slice from the top of a loaf of stale Vienna bread and remove the soft crumbs. Fill with oysters seasoned with salt, pepper, and tomato catsup ; dot with bits of butter ; replace the top and bake in a hot oven, basting frequently with the oyster liquor.

**Oyster Macaroni.** — Boil macaroni in a cloth to keep it straight. Put a layer in a dish seasoned with pepper, salt, and butter, then a layer of oysters, until the dish is full. Mix some grated bread with a beaten egg, spread over the top, and bake.

**Oyster Omelet, No. 1.** — Chop one dozen large, fresh oysters in small pieces, sprinkle half a teaspoonful of salt over them, and let them stand in their own liquor, in a cool place, for half an hour. Beat six eggs, the yolks and whites apart ; the former to smooth paste, the latter to a solid froth. Add to the yolks a tablespoonful of rich, sweet cream, pepper and salt in sufficient quantity, and then lightly stir in the whites. Put an ounce and a half of butter in a hot frying-pan, and when it is thoroughly melted, and begins to fry, pour in the egg mixture, and add as quickly as possible the oysters. Do not stir, but with a long-bladed omelet knife lift, as the eggs set, the omelet from the pan, to prevent its scorching. In five minutes, it will be done. Place a hot dish, bottom upward, over the omelet, and dexterously turn the pan over, having the brown side of the omelet uppermost upon the dish. Serve without delay.

**Oyster Omelet, No. 2.** — One dozen large oysters or two dozen small ones chopped fine, six eggs, one cup of milk, one tablespoonful of butter, one teaspoonful of chopped parsley, a dash of pepper and a pinch of salt; beat the yolks and whites of eggs separately; mix the yolks, oysters and seasoning, cook in a frying-pan in the hot butter till the eggs thicken but are not set, then stir in the stiffly beaten whites. Cook a moment longer and slip off on to a hot platter. Serve at once.

**Oyster Omelet, No. 3.** — Allow for every six large oysters or twelve small ones one egg; remove the hard part and mince the rest very fine; take the yolks of eight eggs and whites of four, beat till very light, then mix in the oysters; season and beat up thoroughly; put into a skillet a gill of butter, let it melt; when the butter boils, skim it and turn in the omelet; stir until it stiffens; fry light brown; when the under side is brown, turn on to a hot platter. To brown the upper side, hold a red hot shovel over it.

**Panned Oysters, No. 1.** — Put one tablespoonful butter in a covered saucepan with one-half saltspoonful of white pepper, one teaspoonful salt, and a few grains of cayenne, when hot add one pint of washed and drained oysters, cover closely and shake the pan to keep them from sticking; cook about three minutes or until plump. Serve on toasted bread or crackers.

**Oysters Panned in the Shell, No. 2.** — Wash the shells and wipe dry. Place them in a pan with the round shell down. Set in a hot oven for three minutes; then take out and remove the upper shell. Put two or three oysters into one of the round shells, season with pepper and salt, add butter the size of two peas, and cover with cracker or bread crumbs. Return to the oven and brown.

**Panned Oysters, No. 3.** — Pick over the opened oysters to remove bits of shell. Wash quickly in cold water and drain on sieve. Put into saucepan with one tablespoonful butter for twenty-five oysters and a dash of salt and pepper. Cover and shake over a hot fire until edges ruffle and oysters are plump. May be served on toast.

**Oyster Patties, No. 1.** — Work one ounce of butter and one tablespoonful of flour into a smooth paste. When warm, add a little ground mace, salt, and cayenne. Gradually stir in three tablespoonfuls of cream. Boil for three or four minutes, then pour in the strained liquor of two dozen small oysters. Lastly, add the oysters. Stir for a few minutes and fill patties prepared as follows: Line some patty pans with thin puff paste, fill with rice so they will keep their shape, cover the top with another piece of pastry. Bake in brisk oven. When baked, take off the top, empty out the rice, fill with the oysters, which have been kept warm, replace cover, and serve.

**Oyster Patties, No. 2.** — Put one quart of oysters in a saucepan, with liquor enough to cover them, set it on the stove and let them come to a boil; skim well, and stir in two table-spoonfuls of butter, a little pepper, and salt. Line some patty-pans with puff-paste, fill with oysters, cover with paste, and bake twenty minutes in a hot oven. The upper crust may be omitted, if desired.

**Oyster Patties, No. 3.** — One quart oysters, minced fine with a sharp knife; one cup rich drawn butter based upon milk; cayenne and black pepper to taste. Stir minced oysters in drawn butter and cook five minutes. Have ready some shapes of pastry, baked in pattie-pans, then slipped out. Fill these with the mixture; set in oven two minutes to heat, and send to table.

**Pickled Oysters, No. 1.** — Two gallons large oysters, drain and rinse them; put one pint oyster juice in one quart vinegar over fire; scald and skim until clear; add one tablespoonful whole pepper, one tablespoonful cloves, one tablespoonful mace, one even tablespoonful salt; scald a minute, then throw in oysters; let them just come to a boil. The oysters should be pickled day before being wanted, as they grow tough after stand-ing a few days in vinegar.

**Spiced or Pickled Oysters, No. 2.** — Put into a kettle one hundred and fifty large oysters with the liquor; add salt, and simmer till the edges roll or curl; skim them out; add to the liquor one pint of white wine vinegar, one dozen blades mace, three dozen cloves, and three dozen peppercorns; let it come to a boil, and pour over the oysters. Serve with slices of lemon floating in saucer.

**Pickled Oysters, No. 3.** — Wash fifty oysters, put into a saucepan and strain the liquor over them, adding one tablespoonful of pickling spice and half a teaspoonful of salt; cook until the oysters look plump and the edges curl, then add one cup of vinegar, and when the liquid boils turn at once into hot cans and finish as in canning. Store in a dry place.

**To Pickle Oysters, No. 4.** — Two hundred large oysters, half a pint of vinegar, half a pint of white wine, four spoonfuls of salt, six spoonfuls of whole black pepper and a little mace. Strain the liquor, and add the above-named ingredients. Let boil up once, and pour while boiling hot over the oysters. After these have stood ten minutes, pour off the liquor, which, as well as the oysters, should then be allowed to get cold. Put into a jar and cover tight. The oysters will keep some time.

**Pickled Oysters, No. 5.** — Place one hundred good-sized oysters in porcelain-lined kettle, strain the liquor and add also eighteen cloves, half a nutmeg grated, one teaspoonful of allspice, four blades of mace, a little cayenne pepper, one teaspoonful of salt, and two tablespoonfuls of strong vinegar. Stir all thoroughly with a wooden spoon. Put over a slow fire. Take off the fire several times and stir them thoroughly. Just as soon as they come to a boil pour them in a porcelain-lined pan. Let them stand in a cool place. They will be ready to serve the next day.

**Oyster Pie, No. 1.** — Line a dish with a puff paste or a rich biscuit paste, and dredge well with flour; drain one quart of oysters; season with pepper, salt, and butter, and pour into the dish; add some of the liquor; dredge with flour, and cover with a top crust, leaving a small opening in the centre. Bake in a quick oven.

**Oyster Pie, No. 2.** — One quart oysters, drained; pepper, salt, and butter to taste. One quart flour, two tablespoonfuls lard, one tablespoonful salt, mix with water for pie crust. Butter plate, then line pie plate with crust; fill with oysters, seasoned; put over a crust and bake.

**Little Pigs in Blankets, No. 1.** — Season large oysters with salt and pepper. Cut bacon in very thin slices; wrap an oyster in each slice, and fasten with a little wooden skewer.

Heat a frying-pan and put in the " little pigs." Cook just long enough to crisp the bacon. Place on slices of toast that have been cut into small pieces and serve immediately. Do not remove the skewers. This is a nice relish for lunch or tea ; and, garnished with parsley, is a pretty one. The pan must be very hot before the " pigs " are put in. Great care must be taken that they do not burn.

**Pigs in Blankets, No. 2.** — Have at hand oysters, salt, pepper, sliced fat bacon. Clean, and season some nice large oysters with salt and pepper. Wrap each oyster in a slice of thin bacon, pinning it with a toothpick. Cook them until the bacon is crisp.

**Oyster Rarebit.** — Melt two tablespoonfuls of butter in chafing-dish. Stir in one tablespoonful of corn-starch, add one-half pound old cheese and one cup of oysters after first bringing them to a boil in half cup milk. Stir until cheese is melted, then add one tablespoonful Worcestershire, salt and cayenne pepper. When thoroughly mixed add cup of whipped cream, and serve on toast.

**Oysters in Ramekins.** — Cut round slices of bread to fit your ramekin dishes, the slices not more than a quarter of an inch thick. Toast and butter the slices and lay them in the dishes. Pour over them a little of the oyster liquor to moisten but not make too soft. Dip oysters in melted butter seasoned with salt, pepper, and lemon juice, and lay in each ramekin as many oysters as they will hold. Cover with a thin layer of cream sauce and buttered crumbs, place in a pan in the oven and bake until the crumbs are nicely browned — about twenty minutes. Serve at once.

**Oyster Relish** (*Chafing-dish.*) — One cup oysters (drained), one cup bread crumbs, one egg, one cup milk, one teaspoonful salt, dash cayenne. All the ingredients are placed in dish and stirred together, first beating the egg well. Be very careful in stirring not to break the oysters, and let the mixture stand for a time to swell bread crumbs. Heat a tablespoonful of butter in the chafing-dish, and stir in the mixture and cook until oysters are well curled, then add a little butter.

**Oyster Stew, No. 1.** — Boil one cup of strained oyster-liquor and half a cup of water. Skim, add half a teaspoonful of salt, half a saltspoonful of pepper, one tablespoonful of butter, and one tablespoonful rolled cracker. When it begins to boil add one quart of oysters. Boil one minute. Put half a cup of cream or cold milk into the tureen and pour the boiling stew over it.

**Stewed Oysters, No. 2.** — Pick over and wash one quart oysters. Scald one pint milk. Strain, boil, and skim oyster liquor; when clear add oysters. Cook till oysters are plump and well ruffled; take from fire, add hot milk, salt, and pepper.

If desired thicker, rub together one tablespoonful each of butter and flour; add to milk and stir until smooth. This may be varied by addition of a little chopped celery or onion.

**Stewed Oysters a la Baltimore, No. 3.** — Open neatly three dozen oysters. Place them in a saucepan *without their liquor* and add one ounce of good butter. Cover the pan and place it over the fire. Cook for two minutes. Then add one wine-glass of good Madeira wine and a very little cayenne pepper. Cook together a little longer and then add one gill of espagnole sauce and one-half a glass of demiglazed sauce. Stir thoroughly until it comes to a boil. Just before serving add the juice of one lemon, one teaspoonful of butter, one teaspoonful of finely chopped parsley. Serve immediately in a tureen.

**Steamed Oysters.** — Procure oysters in the shell. Wash them thoroughly and arrange in a steamer, flat side up. Cover closely, place over boiling water and let steam about twenty-five minutes. When the shells open, the oysters are done. Remove the lower shells, put a bit of butter on each, sprinkle with pepper and salt, garnish with cut lemon and serve hot on hot plates.

**Shirred Oysters.** — Chop twenty-five oysters, add the beaten yolks of two eggs, pepper and salt to taste, two tablespoonfuls of cream and dry bread crumbs to thicken. Fill the shells with this mixture and brown in the oven.

**Scalloped Oysters, No. 1.** — Clean one pint of medium-sized oysters. Moisten one teacup of cracker crumbs with one-third of a cup of melted butter. Spread one-quarter of the crumbs in a baking dish, over them put one-half of the oysters, season with salt, white pepper, and lemon juice. Then spread another quarter of a cup of the crumbs, then the remaining oysters. Season again with salt, pepper, and lemon juice, and cover with the remaining crumbs. Bake in quick oven until the liquor bubbles and the crumbs are brown.

**Scalloped Oysters, No. 2.** — One quart solid oysters, cleaned and drained, one-half cup butter, one cup grated bread crumbs, one cup coarse cracker crumbs. Rub the pudding pan thickly with cold butter and sprinkle a layer of bread crumbs, moisten the rest of the bread with part of the butter melted and stir the rest of the butter into the cracker. Arrange oysters and bread in alternate layers, using cracker for the top. Season each with pepper and salt, allowing one and one-half teaspoonfuls of salt, one saltspoonful of pepper, and about one tablespoonful of lemon juice for the whole. Pour over one-quarter cup of the oyster liquor and set aside for an hour. If it looks very dry add another one-quarter cup of oyster juice before baking. Cook about twenty-five minutes in a quick oven. Wine, milk, or Worcestershire sauce are sometimes used, but are no improvement. One suspects that the oysters are not fresh when disguised by such high seasoning.

**Scalloped Oysters, No. 3.** — Cover the bottom of a baking dish (well buttered) with a layer of crumbs, and wet these with cream, put on spoonful by spoonful. Pepper and salt, and strew with minute bits of butter. Next, put in the oysters, with a little of their liquor. Pepper them, stick bits of butter in among them, and cover with dry crumbs until the oysters are entirely hidden. Add more pieces of butter, very small, and arrange thickly on top. Set in the oven, invert a plate over it to keep in the flavor, and bake until the juice bubbles up to the top. Remove the cover, and brown on the upper grating for two or three minutes. Serve in the baking dish.

**Scalloped Oysters, No. 4.** — Open the shells, setting aside for use the deepest ones. Have ready some melted butter, not hot, seasoned with minced parsley and pepper. Roll each oyster in this, letting it drip as little as may be, and lay in the shells, which should be arranged in a baking pan. Add to each a little lemon juice, sift bread crumbs over it, and bake in a quick oven until done. Serve in the shells.

**Scalloped Oysters, No. 5.** — Make a cream sauce, using a pint of milk; pour a little into a buttered pudding dish, add a layer of oysters, sprinkle with bread crumbs seasoned with salt and pepper and dotted with butter; add another layer of sauce, then oysters, crumbs, and butter; repeat this process until the dish is full, having crumbs and dots of butter on top. Bake in a moderate oven. Cerealine or cracker crumbs may be used instead of bread crumbs, and a grating of cheese on top is often an improvement. Sprinkle lightly with chopped parsley before sending to the table. Serve with olives.

**Scalloped Oysters, No. 6.** — Pick, wash, and drain one solid quart oysters. Put in layers in baking dish, alternating with dry bread or cracker crumbs and seasoning. When dish is filled add strained oyster liquor and sufficient milk to moisten. Cover with crumbs, add one tablespoonful butter in bits, and bake one-half hour in hot oven.

**Stuffed Oysters.** — Have at hand twenty-eight large oysters and some chicken forcemeat prepared as follows: Scrape and pound the breast of an uncooked medium-sized fowl, then rub it through a puree sieve. Mix one-quarter of a cup of cream or milk with one-eighth of a cup of fine bread crumbs. Cook them slowly until they form a smooth paste. Then add the chicken, the white of one egg, one tablespoonful of butter, one-half teaspoonful of salt, a bit of white pepper. Mix all together thoroughly and set away to cool. Dry the oysters thoroughly and season them with salt and pepper. Roll them in bread crumbs. Arrange the forcemeat in half as many pieces as you have oysters and at a corresponding size. Place a piece on fourteen oysters, cover with the remaining oysters. Press them together so they will stick. Take one whole egg and the yolk left from the forcemeat. Beat it well, season with a little salt. Dip each oyster in the egg, then roll them in bread crumbs. Have them well covered with egg and crumbs. Fry in hot fat until a good color. Drain on brown paper and serve very hot with Madeira sauce in a separate dish.

**Oysters Roasted in the Shell, No. 1.** — Wash the shells clean and wipe dry. Place in a baking pan and put in a hot oven for about twenty minutes. Serve on hot dishes the moment they are taken from the oven. Though this is not an elegant dish, many people enjoy it, as the first and best flavor of the oysters is retained in this manner of cooking. The oysters can, instead, be opened into a hot dish and seasoned with butter, salt, pepper, and lemon juice.   They should be served immediately.

**Oysters Roasted in the Shell, No. 2.** — Wash and scrub the shells.   Cook in hot oven, on top of stove, over red-hot coals, or in steamer until shells open.   Always place them round shell down to retain juice.   Serve melted butter and vinegar or lemons with them.

**Roasted Oysters.** — Take oysters in the shell; wash the shells clean, and lay them on hot coals; when they are done they will begin to open.   Remove the upper shell, and serve the oysters in the lower shell, with a little melted butter poured over each, and season to taste.

**Raw Oysters.** — Raw oysters are best served in their own shells, on plates of cracked ice.   Blue points are the favorite.   A square block of ice, with the centre melted out and surrounded by a wreath of parsley, makes a pretty receptacle for raw oysters. They may be served without the shells, on beds of cracked ice, or in the oyster plates which have shell-like depressions, with a place for ice in the centre.   Salt, red pepper and quarters of lemon are served with this dish.

**Oysters on the Half Shell.** — Keep on ice till serving time. Have small soup plates half full of fine ice and lay the oysters in the deep half of the shell, on the plates as fast as opened.   Salt, pepper, and a cut lemon should be served at the side, and a true oyster lover will use no other sauce.   Small oysters are preferred, and four to six are enough for each plate.

**On a Block of Ice.** — Have the dealer chip in a ten-pound block of perfectly clear ice a cavity large enough to hold as many oysters as are to be served.   Clean and drain them as usual, but do not season, as it causes the juice to flow.   Fold a large towel and cover it with a napkin to lay in the platter; prop the block of ice carefully with wads of cloth, lest it should tilt in melting.   Fill the platter full of parsley, so that the ice should seem to be resting on green leaves only, and garnish the edge of the oysters with fine small sprigs of parsley and celery tips.

**Oyster Salad, No. 1.** — Scald oysters until they are plump, and then put them in cold water while they are boiling hot, so as to make them firm. Put them to one side and boil five eggs hard. Take off the whites and chop very fine. Lay a bed of white lettuce in a long dish. Place the oysters on this. Cover the oysters with a mayonnaise dressing. Over them place the yolks of the eggs, which have been mashed very fine, and lastly the chopped whites of the eggs. Do not let it stand very long before serving. If you do the oysters and mayonnaise will become watery. Be sure the lettuce is thoroughly dried.

**Oyster Salad, No. 2.** — First bring to a boil one pint of oysters, drain from liquor, and when cold mix with two stalks of celery cut in fine pieces ; place on a bed of lettuce leaves or water-cress and serve with mayonnaise dressing and crisped crackers.

**Oyster Salad, No. 3.** — Bring to a boil four dozen small oysters, in their own liquor, skim and strain ; season with a little salt, pepper, and vinegar ; when cold add about half the quantity of chopped celery and a cup of salad cream, garnish the dish with celery leaves and thin slices of lemon sprinkled with parsley over the top.

**Oyster Sauce.** — Strain fifty oysters ; put the juice into a saucepan ; add one pint of new milk ; let it simmer, and then skim off whatever froth may rise. Rub a large spoonful of flour and two of butter together ; stir this into the liquor ; add a little salt and pepper. Let this simmer five minutes, but do not add the oysters till just as they are to be sent to the table, as oysters much cooked are hard. For turkeys, etc., this is a splendid dressing.

**Oyster Shortcake.** — Boil one quart oysters in their own liquor. As soon as scum is set, remove it and drain and return one pint of liquor to saucepan. Mix scant tablespoonful of flour with two heaping tablespoonfuls of butter. When the mixture is light and creamy, gradually turn upon it the boiling liquor and season with salt and pepper. After boiling up once, stir in three tablespoonfuls of cream, also the oysters. Stir over the fire one-half minute. Serve immediately. Have shortcake ready to fill.

**Spindled Oysters.** — For six persons take two dozen large oysters, two ounces bacon and six small slices of thin toast. Six slender steel skewers will be needed. Cut two dozen wafers of bacon. Fill the skewers with bacon and oysters alternately, running the skewer cross-grain through the muscle of the oyster and stringing the bits of bacon by one corner so that each slice may overlie an oyster; do not crowd them. Lay the skewers across a baking pan and cook under gas or in a quick oven for five minutes. Do not take the oysters from the spindle, but lay each one on a slice of toast, pour over them the drip from the pan and serve at once.

**Oysters Baked on Toast.** — Butter squares of toast and lay them, butter side down, on a platter. Lay the oysters on the toast, bring the liquor to a boil with a tablespoonful of butter, season with salt and pepper, and strain it over the oysters and toast. Put the platter into a hot oven until the edges of the oysters ruffle. Serve on the same dish with slices of lemon.

**Roasted Oysters on Toast.** — Eighteen large oysters, or thirty small ones, half a pint of cream, one teaspoonful of flour, one tablespoonful of butter, salt, pepper, three slices of toast. Have the toast buttered and on a hot dish. Put the butter in a small saucepan, and when hot add the flour. Stir until smooth, but not brown; then add the cream and let it boil up once. Put the oysters (in their own liquor) into a hot oven for three minutes; then add them to the cream. Season and pour over the toast. Garnish the dish with thin slices of lemon and serve very hot. It is nice for lunch or tea.

**Oyster Toast.** — Select fifteen plump oysters; mince them, and season with mixed pepper and a pinch of nutmeg; beat the yolks of four eggs and mix them with half a pint of cream. Put the whole into a saucepan and set it over the fire to simmer till thick; stir it well, and do not let it boil, lest it should curdle. Toast five pieces of bread, and butter them; when your dish is near the boiling point, remove it from the fire and pour it over the toast.

**Plain Oyster Soup.** — Pour a quart of oysters in colander, rinse by pouring over them a pint cold water. Put this in a porcelain kettle, add a pint boiling water, let boil, skim thoroughly, season with pepper and piece butter size of large egg. Then add oysters, having removed all shells; let boil up once, season with salt and serve.

# CLAMS.

Thin shell clams (soft shells) and round shell clams (quahaugs) furnish a delicious and wholesome form of food if eaten only when fresh. They are more easily opened and have a finer flavor when cooked in the shells.

There is no special season for these most nutritious fish, but custom decrees that they shall be served only during the season when oysters are forbidden. Most of the methods of serving oysters can be applied with slight modification to the cooking of clams.

**A Clam Bake.** — An impromptu clam bake may be had at any time at low tide along the coast where clams are found. If you wish to have genuine fun, and to know-what an appetite one can have for the bivalves, make up a pleasant party and dig for the clams yourselves. A short, thick dress, shade hat, rubber boots, — or, better still, no boots at all, if you can bring your mind to the comfort of bare feet, — a small garden trowel, a fork, and a basket, and you are ready. Let those who are not digging gather a large pile of driftwood and seaweed, always to be found along the shore. Select a dozen or more large stones, and of them make a level floor ; pile the driftwood upon them, and make a good brisk fire to heat the stones thoroughly. When hot enough to crackle as you sprinkle water upon them, brush the embers off, letting them fall between the stones. Put a thin layer of seaweed on the hot stones, to keep the lower clams from burning. Rinse the clams in salt water by plunging the basket which contains them in the briny pools nearby. Pile them over the hot stones, heaping them high in the centre. Cover with a thick layer of seaweed, and a piece of old canvas, blanket, carpet, or dry leaves to keep in the steam. The time for baking will depend upon the size and quantity of the clams. Peep in occasionally at those around the edge. When the shells are open the clams are done. They are delicious eaten from the shell with no other sauce than their own briny sweetness. Melted butter, pepper, and vinegar should be ready for those who wish them ; then all may " fall to." Fingers must be used. A Rhode Islander would laugh at any one trying to use a knife and fork. Pull off the thin skin, take them by the black end, dip them in the prepared butter, and bite off close to the end. If you swallow them whole they will not hurt you. At a genuine Rhode Island clam bake, bluefish, lobsters, crabs, sweet potatoes, and ears of sweet corn in their gauzy husks are baked with the clams. The clam steam gives them a delicious flavor. Brown bread is served with the clams, and watermelon for dessert completes the feast.

**Baked Soft-shell Clams.** — Select as many soft-shell clams as are desired. Be sure to get very large ones. Scrub the shells clean. Then remove the string and loosen the clam from the shell, leaving it as nearly whole as possible. Season each clam in its shell with pepper and a little butter. Then place a very thin slice of pork over each one and replace the other half of the shell. Set them in a pan and bake in a moderate oven until thoroughly steamed.

**Clam Broth.** — Twenty-five clams washed and drained, steam till the shells open easily ; save every drop of juice that comes with opening and add enough water to make one quart. With a pair of scissors trim off the soft part of the clam and reserve to serve with the broth. Chop the tough portion a little and simmer fifteen minutes in the broth. Strain and add pepper and salt if needed and serve in very small bouillon cups. Send the reserved portion to the table with melted butter and lemon juice poured over them.

**Clam Bisque, No. 1.** — Boil one quart of opened clams for twenty minutes in three pints of good veal consomme. Strain and add two tablespoonfuls of butter, two tablespoonfuls of blended flour, and one pint of cream. Cook for a few minutes. Then stir in the well-beaten yolks of four eggs. Cook for a few minutes longer. Season with salt and white pepper to taste.

**Clam Bisque, No. 2.** — Wash two quarts soft-shelled clams, put in a kettle with one-half cup hot water, cover, and cook until shells open. Drain the liquor from clams and strain through a double thickness of cheesecloth. Add enough boiling water to make one quart liquid. Cook one tablespoonful finely cut onion and two tablespoonfuls grated carrot in two tablespoonfuls butter five minutes. Add two tablespoonfuls flour and stir until well blended, then pour on gradually while stirring constantly the clam liquor. Bring to the boiling point, strain and add one cup cream, and the yolks of two eggs beaten slightly. Season with salt, pepper, and a slight amount of powdered nutmeg.

**Clam Chowder, No. 1.** — One quart of opened hard clams, drained and chopped very fine, two dozen soft-shelled clams, chopped in the same way, with the hard part removed. Cut one quart of peeled potatoes in small squares. Bruise and steep one-half pound of hard crackers in cold water. Chop two large white onions and two ounces of salt pork very fine. Put the pork and onion in a stew-pan with one ounce of butter. Fry until a light brown, add the potatoes, six peeled and sliced tomatoes, one quart of water, three pints of white broth, veal or chicken, ground thyme, mace, sage, and white pepper to taste. Boil thirty minutes. Then put in the clams with their liquor and the crackers. Boil thirty minutes longer. Skim the fat, add four ounces of butter, and chopped parsley, mix thoroughly, and serve at once.

**Clam Chowder, No. 2.** — Forty-five clams chopped, one quart of sliced potatoes, one-half pint sliced onions. Cut a few slices of salt pork, fry to a crisp, chop fine. Put in kettle a little fat from the pork, a layer of potatoes, clams, onions, a little pepper and salt ; another layer of chopped pork, potatoes, etc., until all are in. Pour over all the juice of the clams. Cook three hours, being careful not to burn. Add a teacup of milk just before serving.

**Clam Chowder, No. 3.** — Twenty-five clams cut up, one-half pound salt pork chopped fine, six potatoes sliced thin, four onions sliced thin. Put pork in kettle ; after cooking a short time add potatoes, onions, and juice of clams. Cook two and one-half hours, then add clams ; fifteen minutes before serving add two quarts milk.

**Clam Cocktail.** — Open twelve small clams carefully and place the clams and their juice in a basin to allow any sand or shell to settle, then carefully remove them to another bowl and place them on ice. When they are thoroughly chilled, add sufficient catsup to fill four glasses about as large as claret glasses, one small teaspoonful of grated horse-radish, three shakes of tabasco sauce, one tablespoonful of vinegar, and the iced clams. Sometimes one-half teaspoonful of grated onion is added. Serve very cold.

**Clam Croquettes.** — Drain thoroughly and cook two quarts of opened clams until tender with an ounce of butter, a little broth, white pepper, and ground mace — mace may be omitted. Drain again in a colander. Save the liquid and chop the clams fine. Fry a scant tablespoonful of chopped shallot in two ounces of butter until slightly brown and add one ounce of sifted flour. Mix well and then stir in one pint of the liquid you have saved. Stir and boil five minutes. Then add the yolks of four eggs, a dash of red pepper, the chopped clams, and a little finely chopped parsley. Stir constantly and boil two minutes. Add the juice of one lemon. Turn on a dish to cool. Form the mixture in sixteen oblong pieces. Dip in beaten egg, then in cracker crumbs, and fry a light brown. Drain on a brown paper. Serve with a garnish of fried parsley and quartered lemon.

**Deviled Clams.** — Chop fifty clams very fine ; take two tomatoes, one onion chopped equally fine, a little parsley, thyme, and sweet marjoram, a little salt, pepper, and bread crumbs, adding the juice of the clams until the mixture is of the consistency of sausage ; put it in the shells with a lump of butter on each ; cover with bread crumbs, and bake one-half hour.

**Soft Clams a la Newburg.** — Select forty-five good-sized soft clams. Open them and see that they are free from sand. Take each one separately and with the fingers separate the body from the neck. Take care not to break the body. Reject all the rest. Put them in a saucepan with two ounces of butter, a little white pepper, a wineglassful of Sherry, and two medium-sized truffles cut in fine pieces. Cover them and cook slowly for eight minutes. Mix the yolks of three eggs and one pint of cream, beat for three minutes, and pour over the clams. Shake the saucepan gently for three or four minutes. Do not let the mixture boil and do not stir it. Pour into a hot dish and serve at once.

**Stewed Soft Clams, No. 1** (*Chafing-dish*). — One-half dozen large, soft clams, one teaspoonful of butter, one-half pint of boiled milk, one spoonful of cracker dust ; salt and a dash of cayenne pepper. Trim the rough parts from the clams. Put the butter in the chafing-dish ; when quite hot add the boiled milk, cracker dust, salt and pepper. Simmer three minutes. Serve on hot plates.

**Stewed Clams, No. 2.** — Chop the clams and season with pepper and salt; put in a saucepan butter the size of an egg, and when melted add a teaspoonful of flour; add slowly the clam liquor and then the clams, and cook three minutes; then add half a pint of cream, and serve.

**Clam Scallops.** — Chop fifty clams fine, and drain off in a colander all the liquor that will come away. Mix this in a bowl with a cup of crushed cracker, half a cup of milk, two beaten eggs, a tablespoonful melted butter, half a teaspoonful of salt, a pinch of mace and the same of cayenne pepper. Beat into this the chopped clams, and fill with the mixture clamshells, or the silver or stone-china shell-shaped dishes sold for this purpose. Bake to a light brown in a quick oven and serve in the shells. Serve with sliced lemon.

**Minced Clams on Toast.** — Steam and chop enough clams to make one cupful. Put a tablespoonful of butter in the pan and when melted work in one tablespoonful of flour. Add slowly one-half cup each of clam liquor and cream. Season with pepper, a little salt and cook until smooth. Stir all the time. Add the clams at the last moment. Pour over pieces of toast.

**Quahaug Escalops.** — Wash and chop quahaugs quite fine, butter a baking dish first, put in a layer of cracker crumbs, one tablespoonful of the liquor, add bits of butter, salt and pepper and a layer of quahaugs. Proceed until dish is full, having crumbs on top, moisten with half a cup of milk. Bake about twenty minutes. Salmon baked this way instead of quahaugs is nice.

**Cream Clam Bouillon.** — Wash and scrub thoroughly one dozen clams, put in saucepan with one-half cup cold water; place on fire until shells open. Strain juice through cheesecloth; chop clams fine and place in clam juice. Simmer gently ten minutes; then cool for five minutes. Whip until stiff the white of one egg, add crushed clam shells and stir into clams and juice, boil up and strain. Allow an equal quantity of good rich milk; heat milk in double boiler and add a level tablespoonful of butter and one of flour rubbed to a paste; then add to milk and stir until smooth and thick. Cool for five minutes, then add clam broth, heated and seasoned to taste, with red pepper and salt if necessary. Have ready a cup of thick whipped cream; take broth from fire, add whipped cream and serve at once.

**An Inexpensive Supper Dish.** — Take one pint clams, remove the black, chop clams into small pieces. Butter baking dish, put clams, peppered and salted, into bottom of dish. Cream four large potatoes and lay in on top of clams. Mash three large carrots and season with pepper, salt and butter. Put carrots on top of potatoes and press down well. Sprinkle cracker crumbs and grated cheese on top. Lastly, pour on one-half cup of milk and bake until a golden brown. This dish can be gotten up for twenty-five cents and will serve five people.

# SCALLOPS.

The only edible part of the scallop is the central muscle by which the mollusk opens and closes its shell. Shippers sometimes add saleratus to the scallops to improve their appearance, but this is a detriment to the fish. In buying, avoid the large ones that are white, choosing instead those of medium size and the natural creamy white color. They are most appetizing when fried. Rinse them in salt water, dry in a napkin, and dredge with flour. Fry in very hot pork fat. Eggs and crumbs are not needed.

**Devilled Scallops.** — Put one quart of scallops in a saucepan and heat in their own liquor just to the boiling point. Drain, save the liquor, and chop them rather fine. From one-half of a cup of butter remove one tablespoonful. Beat the contents of the cup to a cream, and add one teaspoonful of salt, one-eighth of a teaspoonful of cayenne, and one teaspoonful of made mustard. Beat thoroughly and mix with one cup of white stock — have it hot. Stir the chopped scallops and their liquor into this sauce and let them stand for half an hour. At the end of that time put them in an escalop dish or shells. Sprinkle with the crumbs, dot with the tablespoonful of butter, and bake in a moderate oven for twenty minutes.

**Fried Scallops, No. 1.** — Wash and dry the necessary amount of scallops. Season them with salt and white pepper. Roll them in fine bread crumbs, then in beaten egg, and again in bread crumbs, then in beaten egg, and again in bread crumbs. Arrange in frying basket so they do not touch each other and plunge in a kettle of boiling fat. Cook until a delicate brown and serve with tartare sauce.

**Fried Scallops, No. 2.** — Wipe dry; dip separately into seasoned egg, then into cracker dust, and fry in hot lard.

**Scallops in Batter.** — Wash and dry large scallops. Dip each in fritter batter (see Fritters) and fry golden brown in smoking-hot fat.

**Scallop Fritters.** — Wash and drain one quart of scallops, season them with salt and white pepper, and mix them with the following batter : one pint of sifted flour, a scant half-pint of milk, one tablespoonful of melted butter or oil, one teaspoonful of salt, and two eggs. Beat the eggs briskly, then add the milk. Beat again and pour the mixture on the flour. Then add the butter and salt. Stir in the scallops. Drop a spoonful at a time of the mixture into boiling fat. Cook until a nice brown. Drain on brown paper and serve very hot.

**Scallops in Shell.** — Drain a pint of them and toss them with a tablespoonful of butter in a saucepan, letting them brown lightly for about ten minutes. Then take them out and chop them fine. Melt a spoonful of butter in a saucepan, add a small onion minced fine and brown it lightly. Then add a heaping teaspoonful of flour and stir in slowly a cup of liquor drained from the scallops. Season with a teaspoonful of salt, a pinch of cayenne, and a little white pepper. Mix with the chopped scallops four tablespoonfuls of bread crumbs and yolks of three eggs, and cook all together for three minutes. Then fill the shells, sprinkle fine bread crumbs over the top and dot with bits of butter, and set them in a hot oven to brown for ten minutes. Serve them on platter with green garnish.

**Scallops with Tartare Sauce.** — Dry scallops after washing, then roll in cracker dust, afterward in egg and crumbs and drop them into boiling fat for a minute, so they will take on a light brown. The crumbs must have salt and pepper mixed with them.

Tartare Sauce. — One-half cup of mayonnaise dressing, six small sour pickles, one quarter bottle of capers, one hard-boiled egg, one medium-sized raw onion, a little green parsley. Chop all together very fine and mix with the mayonnaise dressing.

# LOBSTERS.

The markets are supplied with these delicious shell fish, and they may be obtained in good condition all the year. The canned lobster is also convenient in an emergency, for use in soups and salads. Lobsters are put alive into boiling salt water, and cooked twenty minutes from the time the water boils. They should not be eaten until cold, and never be kept more than eighteen hours after boiling. Lobsters are difficult of digestion, and should be eaten with mustard, cayenne pepper, and lemon juice or vinegar.

When freshly boiled they are stiff, and their tails turn strongly inward; when the fish appear soft and watery, they are stale. The flesh of the male lobster is generally considered of the finest flavor for eating, but the hen lobster is preferred for sauce and soups, on account of the coral.

BE SURE IN ALL CASES TO REMOVE INTESTINAL CORD (BLACK CORD FOUND IN CENTRE OF BACK RUNNING FROM BODY TO END OF TAIL).

**Boiled Lobster.** — To properly boil lobsters, throw them living into a kettle of fast-boiling salt and water, that life may be destroyed in an instant. Let them boil for about half an hour. When done, take them out of the kettle, wipe them clean, and rub the shell with a little salad oil, which will give them a clear red appearance. Crack the large claws without mashing them, and with a sharp knife split the body and tail from end to end. The head, which is never eaten, should also be separated from the body, but laid so near it that the division is almost imperceptible. Dress in any way preferred.

**To Open a Boiled Lobster.** — Wipe off shell, break off large claws; separate tail from body; take body from shell, leaving " lady," or stomach, on shell. Put aside green fat and coral; remove small claws; remove woolly gills from body, break latter through middle, and pick out meat from joints. Crush or cut under side of tail, draw meat from shell. Draw back flesh on upper end and PULL OFF INTESTINAL CORD FOUND IN CENTRE OF BACK. Break edge of large claws and remove meat.

**Broiled Lobster with Sauce.** — Select as many chicken female lobsters as desired. Split them open and remove all the

THE LOBSTER FISHERMAN

fat and coral. Set aside for the sauce. Brush the meat of the lobster with melted butter, and broil over a clear fire. When cooked, place on a platter and pour a little melted butter over each lobster. Set in oven for five minutes, then serve with the following sauce :

*Sauce for Broiled Lobster :* The quantity of sauce depends upon the number of lobsters you have. Mix salt, white pepper, oil, and vinegar, the same as for a plain French dressing, but do not have it quite as strong of the vinegar. Add dry mustard to taste, and the coral and fat of the lobster. Stir constantly over the fire until it comes to a boil. When served it should be as thick as a cream.

### Lobster à la Brooklyn with Sauce and Hominy Croustade.

— Cook two medium-sized lobsters in court bouillon for twenty-five minutes. When cold, cut the shell with sharp scissors, from the head down, taking care not to crack the shell. Have the head and shell joined. Take out the tail and remove the small black vein which runs the entire length. Also remove the small sac at the extreme end. Crack the claws carefully. Take the meat and fat from head and be sure to remove " the lady in the lobster." Remove the coral — should there be any — and set aside for further use. Place the shells and claws in cold water, and make the following forcemeat : Put the lobster through a meat machine. To every cup of lobster have one-half cup of bread crumbs, grated very fine, two tablespoonfuls of white sauce, half a cup of cream, one sherry glass of Madeira wine, and salt and white pepper to taste. Mix all together thoroughly. Fill the shells, dust over with bread crumbs and minute pieces of butter. Bake in moderate oven until a delicate brown. Place on a croustade of hominy, garnish with the claws, and serve with sauce made as follows :

*Sauce for Lobster à la Brooklyn :* Melt one ounce butter, add one tablespoonful of chopped onion, and cook for five minutes. Do not let the mixture brown. Stir in one tablespoonful flour and cook for two minutes. Add half a pint of white stock and cook until it thickens. Remove and strain through a fine sieve. Season to taste and add two wineglasses of Sherry. Serve very hot.

### Lobster à la Bonnefoy (*Waldorf Astoria*).

— Chop up two ounces of onions, and two shallots, fry them in oil without letting them attain a color, and add to them two live lobsters' tails cut in pieces across three-eighths of an inch thick with their shell, saute them for a few moments over a brisk fire, and season with salt, cayenne, a bunch of parsley garnished with thyme and a clove of garlic, moisten with a pint of red or white wine; cover the sautoire, cook the lobsters for fifteen minutes, then drain off the pieces, dress them in a pyramidal form on a dish, and add to the broth a few tablespoonfuls of tomato sauce and espagnole sauce. Pound the creamy parts picked from the body with a little cayenne pepper, press it through a sieve, and stir it into the sauce with some minced mushrooms, pour this over the lobsters, and finish by sprinkling the surface with chopped parsley; and add a little shredded tarragon leaves.

**Lobster Bisque.** — Cover two lobsters weighing about one and one-half pounds each with boiling water. Add one tablespoonful of salt, one head of celery, one small bouquet, half an onion, and six whole peppers. Cook until the lobsters' claws can easily be pulled apart — it will probably take twenty minutes. When cool enough to handle, cut the lobster down the back and remove the meat from the body and claws. Save the coral and the green fat. Put back all the tough part of the small claws and shells, and cook them for twenty minutes in the same liquor. The liquor must be considerably reduced. Dry the coral, then rub it through a sieve. In a saucepan mix one tablespoonful of butter with one ounce of flour. When it comes to a boil, stir in one quart of hot milk. Let this come to a boil. Then add one pint of the lobster broth. This must come to a boil. Then season with salt and white pepper. Stir in the sifted coral enough to give the liquid a bright pink color. Place the green fat and the lobster meat cut in fine pieces in a tureen, pour the hot mixture over them and serve very hot.

**Lobster Chowder.** — Meat of one fine lobster, picked out from the shell and cut into bits, one quart of milk, six Boston crackers split and buttered, one even teaspoonful of salt, one scant quarter teaspoonful of cayenne, two tablespoonfuls of butter rolled in one of prepared flour, a pinch of soda in the milk. Scald the milk, and stir in seasoning, butter, and flour, cook one minute, add the lobster, and simmer five minutes. Line a tureen with the toasted and buttered crackers, dipping each quickly in boiling water before putting it in place, and pour in the chowder.

**Curried Lobster.** — Prepare the lobster as for stew; when it comes to a boil, add a mixture of a heaping teaspoonful of flour, and half a teaspoonful of Indian curry mixed with cold water. Let this boil eight minutes, then serve.

**Lobster Curry.** — Boil a medium-sized lobster, remove the meat, and cut it in small pieces. Make a sauce as follows : three ounces of butter, one tablespoonful of browned flour mixed together over the fire, and two small onions cut in very thin slices. Let this cook a minute or two, then stir in one pint of stock, a little salt, and juice of one lemon, and one tablespoonful of curry dissolved in a little cold water. Boil all together until the mixture thickens, then add the lobster. Have it thoroughly heated, and serve at once with boiled rice in a separate dish.

**Lobster Cutlets.** — Pass the meat from a large lobster through a mincing machine. Place it in a stew-pan and moisten generously with curry sauce. Let it simmer, stirring frequently, for one-half hour. The sauce should be absorbed. Remove from the fire, stir in two eggs, and pour on a flat dish, as deep as you wish your cutlets thick. When cold, form into cutlets with a medium-sized cutter, flour them lightly, dip them in beaten egg, and cover them thickly with fine sifted bread crumbs. Set the cutlets in a cool place for half an hour and then fry in deep boiling fat. Drain on paper. Garnish each one with a small claw and serve.

**Deviled Lobster with Sauce, No. 1.** — Boil two medium-sized lobsters in salted water, to which has been added a little vinegar. When cool, slit them and remove the stony pouch and intestine. Pick all the fat, creamy substance, and coral from the body, tail, and claws, chop very fine. Save the large shells, trim them, and arrange in a pan.

In a saucepan put two tablespoonfuls of chopped shallots with two ounces of butter, and fry until they are dry but not brown. Sprinkle one ounce of flour over them, fry a little longer, then stir in pint of broth. Add the lobster, salt, white pepper, a pinch of cayenne, a little Worcestershire sauce, and two handfuls of moistened and pressed bread crumbs. Stir steadily while all boils five minutes, and add the yokes of four eggs, some chopped parsley, and lemon juice. Mix well, fill the eight prepared shells, sprinkle with bread crumbs, put small bits of butter on top, and bake until slightly brown in a hot oven for eight or ten minutes.

Arrange on a folded napkin, garnish with quartered lemons and serve with the following sauce in a bowl:

*Sauce for Deviled Lobster:* Fry one tablespoonful of chopped shallots in one ounce of melted butter until they are slightly brown, and two ladlefuls of espagnole sauce, one ladleful broth, two tablespoonfuls of mixed mustard, a dash of red pepper, and a little Worcestershire sauce. Stir and boil for five minutes. Press through a napkin and stir in some chopped parsley. Serve hot.

**Deviled Lobster, No. 2.** — Procure a live, heavy lobster; put it in a pot of boiling water, with a handful of salt to it. When done and cold, take out all the meat carefully, putting the fat and coral on separate plates; cut the meat in small pieces, rub the coral to a paste; stir the fat in it with a little salt, cayenne, chopped parsley, essence of anchovies, and salad oil, or melted butter and lemon juice; cut the back of the lobster shell in two, lengthwise; wash clean; stir the lobster and sauce well together; fill the shells; sprinkle bread crumbs and a few bits of butter over the top, set in the oven until the crumbs are brown.

**Lobster en Casserole.** — Rub the inside of a casserole with the cut surface of a clove of garlic. Break the meat of a boiled lobster into large pieces and fry in olive oil, adding a tablespoonful each of chopped onion, carrot, and parsley. Add a bay leaf, a pinch of thyme, and two tablespoonfuls of Sherry. Cook for twenty minutes, then take out the lobster and keep hot. Add to the sauce one-half cup of beef stock and one-half cup of stewed and steamed tomatoes. Simmer for ten minutes, put in the lobster, reheat and serve.

**Fricasseed Lobster.** — Put in the pan one tablespoonful of butter and one-half cup of water, when butter is melted add two cups of lobster chopped fine, when this is hot add one tablespoonful of vinegar, little salt, pepper, mace and mustard, and one well-beaten egg. Stir constantly until the sauce is creamy and thick. Serve piping hot.

**Timbale of Lobster à la Maryland.** — Cook two medium-sized lobsters in court bouillon for twenty-five minutes. Set aside to cool. Break the tail from the head, cut the tail and remove the black vein which runs the entire length, also remove small sac at the end. Remove "the lady" from the head. There is quite a little meat to be found each side near the small claws. Crack the big claws and remove the meat. Cut all the meat into scallops about one-half inch square.

Make a sauce of the following : Boil three eggs until they are hard, remove the yolks while they are hot, and pound to a paste, add one heaping tablespoonful butter which has been rubbed to a cream. When well mixed, add one heaping teaspoonful flour, half a teaspoonful of salt, and a good pinch of cayenne. Mix all thoroughly and place in a saucepan with half a cup of consomme. Let it boil up, then add one glass Madeira wine.

Add the lobster and let it boil two minutes. Remove and set away to cool. Line a large timbale mold with fish forcemeat, decorate your mold with the coral of the lobster, and put on ice to harden. When firm, pour in the centre your lobster mixture, cover over with forcemeat, and put on ice for one hour and thirty minutes before you want it cooked. Place your mold in a pan of water, cover with buttered paper. Bake in medium oven until forcemeat is firm, from twenty-five to thirty minutes. When done, unmold, serve with Maryland sauce in the centre. Fish forcemeat is made the same as for pompano fillets.

**Lobster à la Newburg, No. 1.** — Two pounds of lobster meat, one tablespoonful of butter, one-half tablespoonful of flour, one cup of cream, one teaspoonful of salt, one-fourth of a teaspoonful of cayenne, two tablespoonfuls of Sherry, and the yolks of two eggs. Melt the butter in the chafing-dish and then stir in the flour. When well mixed, add the cream gradually, stirring it constantly. When hot and smooth, add the nicest part of the lobster cut into medium pieces. Cook until the lobster is thoroughly heated. Add the salt, cayenne, and Sherry. Then add the beaten yolks of the eggs and serve at once.

**Lobster à la Newburg, No. 2.** — Take two pounds of boiled lobster and pick all the meat out of the claws. Cut the meat in medium-sized pieces and place in a deep saucepan, with half a pint of Madeira and a good-sized piece of fresh butter ; season with salt, a little nutmeg, and a very little cayenne pepper. Then cook the whole well together for six or seven minutes, keeping the lid on the pan while cooking. Beat in a bowl a pint of sweet cream and the yolks of two eggs ; add to this the lobster. Add also two finely sliced truffles. Pour into a hot tureen and serve very hot.

**Lobster à la Newburg, No. 3.** — Cut the meat of a lobster weighing two or two and one-half pounds in small pieces and heat in saucepan with two rounded tablespoonfuls of butter. Sprinkle with one-half teaspoonful of salt, and a few grains of paprika, and one tablespoonful of Sherry. Pour the yolks of two eggs and one cup of cream over the lobster and stir until thick and smooth. Then add one or two tablespoonfuls more of Sherry, according to taste. Serve at once.

**Lobster à la Newburg, No. 4.** — Remove the meat from a good-sized lobster and cut in small pieces ; melt two large spoonfuls of butter, add the lobster and cook until thoroughly heated ; season with salt and pepper ; cook one minute and add one-third cup thin cream and the yolks of two eggs slightly beaten ; stir until sauce is thickened, then add two tablespoonfuls Sherry wine and one of brandy.

**Lobster Newburg, No. 5.** — Cut the meat of two small lobsters into small thin slices and cook them slowly in four tablespoonfuls of butter for five minutes. Then add one teaspoonful of salt, one saltspoonful of pepper, a speck of cayenne, two tablespoonfuls each of brandy and Sherry, a dash of mace and simmer five minutes longer. Beat well the yolks of four eggs, mix with them one cup cream and pour it over the cooking mixture. Stir constantly for one and one-half minutes, then serve quickly in a warm dish. Garnish with triangles of puff paste.

**Lobster Newburg, No. 6.** — Season one pint diced lobster with one-half teaspoonful salt, dash cayenne, pinch nutmeg. Put in saucepan with two tablespoonfuls butter, heat slowly. Add two tablespoonfuls Sherry ; cook five minutes ; add one-half cup cream beaten with yolks of two eggs, stir until thickened. Take quickly from fire.

**Lobster Patties.** — Proceed as in oyster patties, but use the meat of cold boiled lobster.

**Lobster à la Portland.** — Take off the tails and big claws of three medium-sized live female lobsters. Remove the string which runs through the centre of each tail and cut crosswise in five or six pieces. Crack the claws and place them on a plate. Boil the bodies. Take out the creamy substance and rub it through a sieve with four egg yolks and one-half pint veloute sauce, four chopped shallots, and one bruised clove of garlic. Add two ounces of butter and fry a little without browning. Add the lobster, a bunch of parsley, and pinch of red pepper. Fry a little longer, occasionally tossing the lobster. Add one-half pint of white broth and one-half pint of white wine, and boil fifteen minutes. Remove the bunch of parsley and skim out the lobster. Reduce the liquid, add two ladlefuls of veloute sauce, and the prepared egg yolks. Stir constantly until it nearly boils, add a little chopped parsley and juice of one lemon. Pour the sauce over lobster and serve at once.

**Lobster Salad, No. 1.** — Cut the meat of the lobster in pieces about one inch square. Place them in an earthen bowl and season with a French dressing of olive oil, vinegar, and a little salt and white pepper. Wash and thoroughly dry the white leaves of lettuce. Arrange on a flat dish in the form of shells. Drain the lobster and mix with enough mayonnaise dressing to make it rich and creamy. Fill each shell with it and pour a little mayonnaise on top of each one. Garnish the dish with lettuce leaves.

**Lobster Salad, No. 2.** — Cut the lobster in half-inch cubes, mix with salad cream and arrange in nests of crisp lettuce leaves. If the whole lobster is used, garnish with the grated lobster coral and arrange the small lobster claws about the dish. A little celery salt may be sprinkled upon the lobster if one desires the flavor of celery.

**Lobster Sauce.** — Break the shell of the lobster into small pieces. Pour over these one pint of water or veal-stock and a pinch of salt; simmer gently until the liquid is reduced one-half. Mix two ounces of butter with an ounce of flour, strain the liquid upon it and stir all, over the fire, until the mixture thickens, but do not let it boil. Add two tablespoonfuls of lobster meat chopped fine, the juice of half a lemon, and serve.

**Lobster Soufflé.** — Dice a two-pound lobster, showing the red side as much as possible. Put bands of writing paper, about two inches high, around as many individual ramequin cases as you wish to serve. Beat three tablespoonfuls of stiff mayonnaise, one cup aspic jelly, one-half cup tomato sauce together until they begin to look white, then stir in the pieces of lobster, adding a very little tarragon vinegar, or better still, one teaspoonful chopped tarragon and put away to stiffen in a very cold place. When set, take off the papers carefully, garnish with pounded coral or brown crumbs.

**Lobster à la Somerset.** — Melt one-quarter cup butter, add one tablespoonful flour, one-half teaspoonful salt, a few grains cayenne; pour gradually one cup thin cream, add meat from a good-sized lobster cut in cubes, and when heated add one beaten egg and two tablespoonfuls Madeira wine.

**Steaming Lobsters and Clams.** — Have a large, deep kettle of water boiling rapidly and immerse the lobster. Boil until the shell turns red, when it is done. Be sure to have the receptacle large enough to have the water completely cover the lobster when it is dropped in. Clams are washed and put on a hot stove with just a little water in the bottom of the pan, and as it boils it will steam the clams so that they will open their shells. When the shell opens they are done. Keep the pan covered.

**Stewed Lobster, No. 1.** — Take the meat of two medium lobsters, cut in dice, season with salt as needed, one-half salt-spoonful cayenne, and one-half lemon. Make a white sauce, add another tablespoonful butter and the seasoned lobster; let it simmer ten minutes and serve hot.

**Stewed Lobster, No. 2.** — Boil four medium-sized lobsters in salted water and a generous portion of vinegar. Remove the meat, cut in slices, and arrange in the serving dish. Cover with another dish and keep warm. Make a paste of two ounces of cracker crumbs, six ounces of melted butter, add white pepper, a dash of cayenne, and some chopped parsley. Boil three table-spoonfuls of beef extract with glass of Sherry, gradually stir in the crackers and butter, also the fat of the lobster which has been rubbed through a sieve. Stir in two tablespoonfuls of vine-gar. Do not let the mixture boil after the crackers and butter have been added. Mix well and pour over the lobster. Serve immediately. Should the sauce curdle, add a teaspoonful of water and stir with an egg beater.

**Stewed Lobster, No. 3.** — A middling-sized lobster is best; pick all the meat from the shells and mince it fine; sea-son with a little salt, pepper and grated nutmeg; add three or four spoonfuls of rich gravy and a small bit of butter. If you have no gravy, use more butter and two spoonfuls of vinegar; stew about twenty minutes.

**Lobster Stew, No. 4.** — Melt four tablespoonfuls butter, and add three tablespoonfuls flour mixed with one-half teaspoonful salt and one-eighth teaspoonful pepper; pour on one quart of rich milk when it reaches the boiling point, add two cups of lobster cut in small pieces; cook one minute and serve.

**Lobster Timbale.** — Place two pounds of cooked lobster, half a pound of chicken halibut, and the whites of two eggs in a mortar, pound to a pulp, and then press through a puree sieve. Moisten with one-half cup of Béchamel sauce and half a cup of cream. Beat all together until very light. Season to taste with salt, white pepper, a dash of cayenne, and a little grated nutmeg. Stir thoroughly, then set the mixture away on ice for one hour or more until it cools and stiffens. Then take a small portion, place it in buttered timbale mold, and poach in the oven for about ten minutes. At the end of that time, if not firm to the touch, add the beaten white of one egg to the raw mixture. If too firm to the touch, add more cream to the raw mixture. Then place in buttered mold, cover with buttered paper and poach in the oven until firm to the touch. Serve with Béchamel sauce, or any other desired.

**Lobster on Toast.** — Remove the meat from a good-sized lobster and cut in small pieces; put in the chafing-dish one-half cup hot water, one tablespoonful vinegar, one-half teaspoonful salt, two tablespoonfuls butter, and dash cayenne, and let it boil; then add the lobster and simmer for five minutes; serve on buttered toast.

**Hominy Croustade.** — Place one cup of hominy, one quart of water, and one teaspoonful of salt in a saucepan over the fire. Stir well to free it from lumps and cook for two hours. While hot, pour into mold about one inch deep and the desired size to accommodate the lobsters. Be sure to wet the mold with ice-water before pouring in the hominy. When cool, turn it out on platter it is to be served on. When it is to be warmed, stand the dish over a pan of hot water.

# CRABS.

These are found near the coast of the Southern and Middle States, and are considered such a luxury in Maryland that special means are taken for their propagation. They are usually quite expensive in Eastern markets. Crabs, like lobsters, shed their shell annually. When the new shell is forming, they are called soft-shell crabs, and are highly esteemed by epicures.

The same general rules for inspection as in lobsters.

**Crab Bisque, No. 1.** — Twelve large, hard-shell crabs boiled in salted water. The female crab, known by the light red claws and large flap, is the best. Drain, remove the large shell, but save the creamy part that sticks to it. Put this with the coral that is in the crab, pound fine with four ounces of butter and the yolks of four eggs, and rub through a sieve. Pare off the flaps and gills, wash off the sand, and pound what is left of the crab to a puree. Chop a medium-sized onion, put it in a saucepan with four ounces of butter, fry a minute or two, then add one pound of steeped and pressed white bread and the crab puree. Stir the whole to a paste and gradually stir in one-half pint Catawba wine and enough white broth to make it of the right consistency. Add a bouquet and boil all for one-half hour. Rub through a fine hair sieve, stir and boil again. Add the prepared egg yolks, white pepper and a pinch of cayenne, one-half pint boiling cream. Mix well without boiling and pour into a tureen. If possible, serve with small boiled oyster crabs separately on a plate.

**Crab Bisque, No. 2.** — For eight persons use eighteen large, hard-shell crabs, one quart of chicken or veal stock, one quart of cream, one pint of stale bread free of crust, two tablespoonfuls of butter, one of flour, one small slice of carrot, one large slice of onion, two bay leaves, one stalk of celery, one sprig of parsley, a bit of mace, slight grating of nutmeg, one-fourth teaspoonful of white pepper, dash of cayenne, and three teaspoonfuls of salt. Put one-half the meat of the crabs and all of the claws into a stew-pan. Add the spice, vegetables, herbs, and half the stock, and place the pan where its contents will simmer gently for forty minutes. Ten minutes later put the bread and the remaining stock into another stew-pan, and set the pan where its contents will simmer gently for thirty minutes. When the first mixture has cooked for the proper period, strain it over that in the second stew-pan. Mix all these ingredients thoroughly and rub through a fine sieve. Return to the fire and add butter and flour which have been rubbed together. Cook five minutes longer and add the cream heated in a double boiler, the remainder of the crab meat, salt and pepper. Let the soup boil up once and serve. If one chooses, one tablespoonful of brandy and three of Sherry may be added after the bisque is taken from the stove.

**Crab Canapés.** — Remove all the meat from eighteen hard-shell boiled crabs. Place on a plate, season with a teaspoonful of salt and half a saltspoonful of cayenne. Fry one finely chopped onion in one ounce of butter over a moderate fire for about two minutes, add two tablespoonfuls of flour, and cook two minutes more, then pour in one gill of broth and cook slowly for five minutes. Stir all the time it is cooking Add the crab meat and cook all for fifteen minutes, stirring occasionally. Remove and set away to cool. Mix one tablespoonful of butter and one tablespoonful of flour and cook over a moderate heat for three minutes. Add two ounces of grated Parmesan cheese and two ounces of Swiss cheese, stirring them well together until melted. While it is cooling, cut six good-sized slices of bread about one-quarter of an inch thick, trim off the crust and fry, until a light brown, in a little fresh butter. When cool, spread each slice with a layer of crab meat about one-quarter of an inch thick. Divide the cheese mixture in six equal portions. Shape each into a ball and place in the centre of the crab meat. Put all in a dish and bake in a hot oven for five or six minutes. Serve in the same dish they were in while cooking.

**Deviled Crabs, No. 1.** — One dozen fresh crabs boiled and pickled ; quarter of a pound of fresh butter, one small teaspoonful of mustard powder, cayenne pepper and salt to taste. Put the meat into a bowl and mix carefully with it an equal quantity of fine bread crumbs. Work the butter to a light cream, mix the mustard well with it, then stir in very carefully, a handful at a time, the mixed crabs and crumbs. Season to taste with cayenne pepper and salt, fill the crab shells with the mixture, sprinkle bread crumbs over the tops, put three small pieces of butter upon the top of each, and brown them quickly in a hot oven. They will puff in baking and will be found to be very nice.

**Deviled Crabs, No. 2.** — One cup crab meat, picked from shells of well-boiled crabs, two tablespoonfuls fine bread crumbs or rolled cracker, yolks two hard-boiled eggs chopped, juice of a lemon, one-half teaspoonful mustard, a little cayenne pepper and salt, one cup good drawn butter. Mix one spoonful crumbs with chopped crab meat, yolks, seasoning, drawn butter Fill scallop shells — large clam shells will do — or small pâté-pans — with the mixture; sift crumbs over top, heat to slight browning in quick oven.

**Crab Farcie with Tomato Sauce.** — Take the meat of two crabs to every shell and mix with two and one-half medium-sized slices of bread which have been soaked in bouillon. (Water will do if you have no bouillon.) Press out dry and add one tablespoonful of melted butter, one teaspoonful of dry mustard. Pepper and salt to taste and moisten all with one-half cup of tomato sauce.

**Gumbo of Crabs.** — Take eight large, soft-shell crabs, clean them, and pare off the small legs, flaps, and gills which are spongy and generally sandy. Wash, drain well, and cut each crab in about eight pieces. Put in a saucepan two ounces butter, two chopped shallots, and two ounces of ham cut very small. Fry a little, add one-half pint of white wine, five pints of white broth, salt, pepper, one bunch of parsley tied up with one bay leaf, one sprig of thyme, one clove of garlic, two cloves, one-half a green pepper without the seeds and cut small, and finally the crabs. Cover, and boil slowly for one hour. Remove the parsley, skim the fat, and add six tablespoonfuls of gumbo powder. Drop the powder by the left hand quite a distance from the liquid, all the time stirring with the right hand. This prevents it from getting lumpy. Season highly, pour into a soup tureen, and serve with plain boiled rice on a separate dish.

**Scalloped Crabs.** — Put the crabs into a kettle of boiling water, and throw in a handful of salt. Boil from twenty minutes to a half an hour. Take them from the water when done and pick out all the meat; be careful not to break the shell. To a pint of meat put a little salt and pepper; taste, and if not enough add more, a little at a time till suited. Grate a very little nutmeg, and add one spoonful of cracker or bread crumbs, two eggs well beaten, and two tablespoonfuls of butter (even full); stir all well together ; wash the shells clean, and fill each shell full of the mixture ; sprinkle crumbs over the top and moisten with butter, then bake until nicely browned on top.

**Soft-shell Crabs, No. 1.** — Lift each point of the back shell and remove the spongy substance found beneath it, taking care to scrape and cut away every bit. Turn the crab on its back and remove the semi-circular piece of dark, soft shell called the " apron " or " flap " and more of the same spongy substance lying under it. Wash in cold water and dry carefully on a towel. Season with salt and pepper, dip in egg and roll in crumbs. Fry about three minutes in very hot fat, putting in only two at a time, as they should be ice-cold when prepared. Serve with tartare sauce. Some people like them seasoned only with flour, but most people enjoy the crisp and savory crumbs.

**Soft-shell Crabs, No. 2.** — Season with pepper and salt ; roll in flour, then in egg, then in bread crumbs, and fry in hot lard. Serve hot with rich condiments.

**Fried Soft-shell Crabs, No. 3.** — After cleaning the desired number of crabs, season with salt and pepper, dip in beaten egg, then in fine bread crumbs. Drop in hot fat and cook until crisp and colored a nice brown. Drain and place on hot dish, garnish with sliced lemon and parsley. Serve with tartare sauce or any fried fish sauce desired.

**Timbale of Crabs.** — Cook one dozen hard-shell crabs in boiling water with one onion, a bunch of parsley, a head of lettuce, six peppercorns, blade of mace, two cloves, one bay leaf, and one tablespoonful of salt for ten minutes. Do not boil hard as it toughens the meat. Remove the crabs and set them on a wooden dish to cool. Pick out the meat from the body and claws. Pound well in mortar and rub through puree sieve. Measure your crab meat. There should be one-half pint, good measure. Mix with the meat the well-beaten whites of two eggs. Set away in cool place.

Make the following sauce : One tablespoonful of butter and one of flour. Let them come to a boil. Add one-half cup of milk and one-half cup of liquor the crabs were cooked in, one-half teaspoonful salt, one-fourth teaspoonful white pepper, a good pinch of cayenne. Cook for a few minutes, then stir in the yolks of two eggs, and set away to cool. When cold, add the sauce to the fish with half a cup of whipped cream, measured after the cream is whipped. Set on ice for a few minutes. Decorate some small timbale molds with lobster coral or truffles. Put your forcemeat in, giving it a few knocks on the table to settle forcemeat. Set in ice-box for half an hour. Place the mold in a pan of hot water and cook in the oven for fifteen or twenty minutes or until the forcemeat is firm. Unmold each timbale on a round piece of toast and garnish with the claws and parsley. Put a tablespoonful of Béchamel sauce on each mold and serve the rest in a sauce-boat.

**White House Canapés.** — Chop a medium-sized shallot and fry it lightly without coloring in two ounces of butter. Add a tablespoonful of flour and stir in a pint of cream. Then add one pound of crab meat, salt and pepper, and leave on the fire until it has just begun to bubble. Cut slices of bread one-quarter of an inch thick, trim in any desired shape, either round, oval, or square, and toast on one side only. Put your ingredients on the toasted side of the bread after buttering it with a butter prepared as follows: Mix well together one-quarter of a pound of butter and one-half pound grated Parmesan cheese, and season with red and white pepper. Put the canapés on a buttered dish and slightly brown in the oven.

# SHRIMPS.

Shrimps and prawns are found in the summer season on the Southern coasts. They are similar in form to a lobster, but very small. They should be cooked in boiling salted water from five to eight minutes. Remove the shells and head; the part that is eaten resembles in shape the tail of a lobster. They are used in fish sauces, and are very effective as a garnish.

Shrimp are caught in immense quantities along the seashore from early spring till late autumn, but are chiefly used for bait and for lunches for the parties of children who have unlimited time to pick them from their paper-like shells. If one can take the trouble to pick them out they are really more delicate in fibre and finer flavored than their larger cousins from the gulf. The dainty pink morsels make an appropriate and appetizing garnish for boiled fish of all kinds, and added to any sauce for fish they are more satisfactory than lobster, whose coarser flavor often dominates the fish it is intended to complement. As a curry, or deviled or salad, or in a bisque, they are always good. They may be prepared by any of the formulas already given for lobsters or crabs, remembering that the seasoning should be less heavy as the flavor of shrimp is more delicate. Tinned shrimps should always be rinsed in lightly salted water and well drained and aired before they are used.

**Cosmos Club Shrimps.** — One tablespoonful each of butter and flour creamed. Put in one teacup of sweet cream, add a pinch of red pepper, a little lemon juice and enough tomato sauce to make it the color of shrimps. Put into the chafing-dish and let come to a boil. Add half a pound of shrimps and let boil up once. Serve on hot, buttered crackers.

**Creamed Shrimps.** — The yolks of two eggs, one teaspoonful of anchovy sauce, half a cup of cream, one bottle of shrimps, some slices of toast. Mix in the chafing-dish the yolks of the eggs with the anchovy sauce and cream. Put in the shrimps and let them get thoroughly heated, not allowing the eggs to curdle. Serve on strips of toast.

**Creamed Shrimps Baked with Green Peppers.** — Select twelve even-sized green peppers, remove the stems and seeds, and soak in cold water for three-quarters of an hour. Drain them and stuff with the following mixture: Cream two tablespoonfuls of butter and thoroughly mix it with a quarter of a teaspoonful of pepper, one teaspoonful of mixed mustard, one-eighth of a teaspoonful of celery seed, and one beaten egg. When mixed stir in one cup of fine bread crumbs. Then add one quart of shrimps. Should the shrimps be fresh — not canned ones — you will need to season the sauce with salt. Fill each pepper with the mixture, sprinkle with fine bread crumbs and a piece of butter, and bake in quick oven for fifteen minutes.

**Canapés à la Prince of Wales.** — Take six prawns, six fillets of anchovy, one head of white celery, two gherkins, and two truffles. Cut all into small square pieces about the size of a large pea. Put them into a bowl with enough Prince of Wales sauce to season them thoroughly. Pour nice clear aspic jelly in the bottom of some china cases, then put in the mixtures. Pour some more jelly on the top and set it aside to jell. When wanted, unmold on a platter which has nice white lettuce leaves around the edge. Set individual molds in the centre and garnish with chopped aspic.

**Curried Shrimps.** — Chop fine one small onion and cook until yellow in one and one-half tablespoonfuls butter; add one and one-half tablespoonfuls flour and one-third teaspoonful curry powder; when smooth add one and one-half cups stewed and strained tomato and one can shrimps broken in pieces. Season with salt and pepper or paprika and serve on crackers or toast.

**Dunbar Shrimps.** — Put a big lump of butter in the pan with salt, cayenne, one and one-half teaspoonfuls of table sauce and two cups of cream, when hot add two hard-boiled eggs chopped fine and one pint of shrimps chopped fine; let come to a boil. Serve on hot dainty potato chips or toast.

**Japanese Shrimps.** —- Put a pint of milk in the dish over the hot water pan, when it boils add two tablespoonfuls each of butter and flour creamed and stir till thick, add one cup of strained tomatoes, one-quarter teaspoonful of soda, seasoning, and last the picked shrimps. Serve on toast.

**Shrimp and Peas.** — Melt four tablespoonfuls butter, and add three tablespoonfuls flour mixed with one-half teaspoonful salt and one-eighth teaspoonful pepper; pour on gradually one and one-half cups milk; as soon as sauce thickens add one can shrimp broken in pieces and one can of canned peas, drained from their liquor and thoroughly rinsed.

**Shrimp Salad.** — Take one can of shrimps, take one bunch of lettuce and two stalks of celery, cut up fine, add half a cup of salad cream and mix thoroughly together; pour a little more dressing over the top; garnish edge of platter with pickled beets and lettuce leaves; sprinkle over with chopped parsley and serve.

# Why We Are Successful

THE FREEMAN & COBB COMPANY has been established for nearly thirty-nine years and during that period they have consistently striven to produce a particular standard of Quality. We have surrounded ourselves with an organization that is as near perfection as human ingenuity can make it, having installed the most modern and scientific methods in handling and distributing stock, so that it will reach the dealer in a most attractive and desirable manner.

The great volume of business we enjoy has given us opportunities of perfecting the finest methods possible. Consequently our success has been assured from the start, and the trade has demonstrated this more extensively each year by giving us a steadily increasing business. We are now in a better position to help you increase your business than ever before. We are closely connected with one of the most up-to-date Commission Houses, and the best appointed exclusive Fish Freezer in the business, which are in close touch with leading shippers everywhere, thus enabling us to produce the choicest stock at all times, so we may continually cry " Quality."

We wish especially to call your attention to our " Wachusett Haddies." They are smoked from strictly fancy, carefully selected Shore Haddock and cured by scientific methods and in accordance with all Pure Food Laws, so as to produce a most appetizing, wholesome and nutritious delicacy.

What more can you ask to inspire your confidence than this? We thank you for your loyal support and not only wish you success and prosperity, but trust we will continue to merit a good share of your patronage.

**Freeman & Cobb Co., Inc.**

# WACHUSETT HADDIES

**Famous**

**for their**

**Quality**

**Choicest**

**of the**

**Choice**

## They are different

## WACHUSETT HADDIES—They are different

BECAUSE they are smoked from strictly fancy, carefully selected Shore Haddock, and cured by the most scientific and sanitary methods where all the requirements of the Pure Food Law are observed, producing a most delicious, wholesome and nutritious Haddie. Where supreme excellence is maintained by quality there is brought out the delightful flavor that appeals to the connoisseur.

They are packed in bay leaves and parchment paper in dust proof and attractive boxes containing thirty and fifty pounds.

Increased facilities have enabled us to successfully handle your orders whether large or small and our Haddies are the only Haddies that bear a name and registered trade mark.

Order by the name. Accept no substitute. Demand Wachusett Haddies.

The recipes for Wachusett Haddies are used by permission of
Freeman & Cobb Co., owners of the copyright.

Boston, Mass.,

October 8, 1910.

Freeman & Cobb Co.,

Gentlemen:

I mail you today manuscript recipes
which you ordered.

In using your Wachusett Finnan Haddies,
in the preparation of these recipes, I
have been greatly pleased with the fine
flavor and quality.

Yours truly,

Mary J. Lincoln.

*Author Boston Cook Book.*

# PREPARING WACHUSETT HADDIES

## GENERAL DIRECTIONS

Wachusett Haddies, being only slightly salted before being smoked, need no soaking. Simply wash in lukewarm water, trim off tail and fins, lay the fish in a large shallow pan, cover with boiling water and keep it at just below the boiling point for about fifteen minutes, or until the flakes are white and cooked.

If boiled rapidly, or cooked too long it will be hard and dry. Drain, remove the skin and large or back-bone and unless to be served whole remove the fine bones also and separate into its natural flakes.

If the fish is to be served plain, simply heat again after a slight scalding in hot water or milk to moisten, add butter, pepper and lemon juice and serve.

\*     \*     \*

# WACHUSETT HADDIE SALAD

After scalding the Haddie cool it and separate into flakes. Use equal parts of thinly sliced cold boiled potatoes and the flaked Haddie and dress it to taste with salt, pepper, olive oil and tarragon vinegar; or use any preferred mayonnaise dressing.

\*     \*     \*

# CREAMED WACHUSETT HADDIE

## FOR THE CHAFING DISH

Wash, scald, trim and flake, or use any remnants of broiled or baked Haddie. For one cup of fish flaked, allow one cup of white sauce.

Melt one rounded tablespoon of butter in a small saucepan, or in the blazer of the chafing dish, stir in one rounded tablespoon of flour and add gradually one cup of hot milk (or use half milk and half strained tomato, or use thin cream).

Stir till thick and smooth, add one-fourth teaspoon salt and a dash of cayenne and one teaspoon of lemon juice. Add the flaked fish and when hot serve on toast or with baked potatoes; or put the mixture in a baking dish, or in ramekins, cover with buttered cracker crumbs and bake till brown.

To vary this method, cook one teaspoon each of minced onion and sweet green pepper (or the canned red pimento) in the butter before adding the flour. Or add one beaten egg to the sauce just before serving, cooking it only enough longer to set the egg, and serve like picked up Codfish. Or add one-fourth cup of grated cheese to the sauce to make up for the smaller amount of nutriment in the fish when dried.

# WACHUSETT HADDIE IN GREEN PEPPERS

Cook one teaspoon of minced onions in a rounded tablespoon of hot butter, slowly, till cooked but not browned; add one tablespoon of flour, mix, then stir in gradually one-half cup each of thin hot cream and strained tomato, add one-fourth teaspoon of salt, stir in one cup of scalded and flaked Haddie. Divide three sweet green peppers from stem to small end making boat shapes; remove seeds and white fibre and fill with the mixture, cover with cracker crumbs moistened in melted butter, put them in a shallow pan close together and half cover with hot water, add one tablespoon of butter to the water and bake about twenty minutes or till brown.

\* \* \*

# WACHUSETT HADDIE—Scorched or Toasted

As a relish for supper, a bit of scalded and drained Haddie may be slightly toasted over gas, or laid directly on the hot coals for a minute's browning, or quickly browned in hot butter, in the chafing dish.

\* \* \*

# WACHUSETT HADDIE—Baked

Wash, scald, trim, remove skin and bone if you like, but leave the fish whole.

Lay it in a shallow baking-pan and nearly cover with milk. Bake about twenty minutes, basting frequently with the milk. If liked richer use thin cream and cover the fish with a sprinkling of minced onion, sweet green pepper and tomatoes, then with cracker crumbs, and bake until well browned.

\* \* \*

# WACHUSETT HADDIE a la Tarragona

Prepare one cup of scalded and flaked Haddie, saute it in one rounded tablespoon of butter in the blazer, add a dash of cayenne and one tablespoon of tarragon vinegar and stir while it heats. Dilute one beaten egg with one cup of hot thin cream and after setting the blazer over the hot water pan to prevent the egg curdling stir in the mixture and cook until the egg is set, stirring constantly, salt to taste and serve at once. If you approve of using sherry instead of the vinegar the dish may be called *a la Newburgh*.

# WACHUSETT HADDIE — Broiled

Wash, scald, trim, drain and wipe dry. Remove the large bone, keeping the fish whole if possible. Spread generously with softened butter and lay it on a wire broiler well greased with a bit of pork rind. Broil flesh side first, for about five to eight minutes, then brown the skin side until slightly scorched. Scrape off the skin, turn the fish onto a hot platter and moisten slightly with hot water or milk, and butter; or with thin cream. Add lemon juice and pepper if liked.

Haddock being in its fresh state a dry fish, with no fat, needs after curing a rich sauce or a generous moistening with milk and butter, or cream to make it at its best, especially when it is to be broiled, as this method often makes the fish still more dry.

\* \* \*

# WACHUSETT HADDIE SALAD No. 2

Take equal parts of finely minced cucumbers and prepared Haddie, moisten with mayonnaise dressing and serve in a tomato cup on a bed of lettuce.

# How Finnan Haddies Originated

 DISCUSSION on the merits of food fishes among a party of men in Boston, and the difference between the flavor of the Scotch and American finnan-haddie, writes Col. Robert Mitchell Floyd, brought out an exclamation from an Americanized Scottish Highlander. "Mon! Mon!" he exclaimed, "but do you know how the findon-haddie happened to be?" We admitted our ignorance. "Many years ago at a seaport town on the North Sea, Port Lethen, a fire occurred in one of the fish-curing houses, and partially burned the end of the structure, which was piled full of lightly salted, freshly caught Haddock, which were lying on beds of dry kelp."

"After the flames were extinguished and the charred top and side of one of the piles of fish were removed, the Maister pulled out one of the slightly smoked Haddock, still warm from the heat. He smelt it, while the curious group of his men around him watched his every move; he tore off a piece of the fish, and tasting it, took another bit, sagely nodded his head, and passed it over to the foreman, Sandy, saying, 'Taste you it, Sandy! It is nae so nasty.' This proved to be a great day in Port Lethen, for every fisherman in the town had a Haddie given him free of cost that had been cured by the smoke from the burning kelp, and from that time until the present no one in Port Lethen, or the greater fishing village a mile away, Findon, ever cured a Haddock except by smoking them over the burning seaweed."

The cleverness of the Findon fish dealers in being the first to put this new cured Haddie on the market won for them the glory of the trade name "findon haddie," which was abbreviated later on into "finnan-haddie."

# Our Products are Unrivaled in Quality

---

**I**F you handle Quality Stock these Haddies will appeal to you. In order to protect our trade from inferior grades we request you to insist on having WACHUSETT HADDIES.

WACHUSETT KIPPERED HERRING are herring specially selected, split, slightly cured and smoked, packed in boxes containing 75 and 100 each.

WACHUSETT BLOATERS are large culled herring, round, slightly salted, smoked and packed in boxes containing 50 and 100 count.

WACHUSETT DEVILED LOBSTER, preparation of the finest parts of the Lobster, ready to serve, can be used for Sandwiches, Soups, Chowders, Newburgh and Canape. Packed in parchment lined cans, case containing eight dozen one-quarter pound size cans.

*We urgently recommend the above products and trust when ordering you will include the entire variety.*

## FREEMAN & COBB CO., Inc.

**BOSTON, MASS.**